# Logic Before Language

Fluency is not intelligence. Prediction is not understanding. And today's AI has mistaken one for the other.

In an era dominated by language models that imitate thought without engaging in it, *Logic Before Language* makes a bold and urgent argument: if we want machines that truly understand, reason, and justify their conclusions, we must rebuild AI from its logical foundations.

Drawing from the intellectual lineage of Aristotle, Euclid, Russell, Gödel, Turing, McCarthy, and Minsky, Martin Milani exposes the core illusion beneath modern AI, the belief that eloquence and probability can substitute for meaning and reasoning. He shows how today's systems generate speech without comprehension, confidence without justification, and predictions without any grounding in truth.

At the center of the book is Real-Time Reasoning (RTR), a new multi-layer architecture for AI that integrates perceptual learning with Bayesian inference, symbolic reasoning, fuzzy logic, logic-based explanation, and transparent decision pathways. RTR does not imitate intelligence; it constructs it. It reasons in real time, exposes every inference step, and produces conclusions that can be interrogated, audited, verified, and trusted.

This architecture is designed for epistemic integrity, with systems that not only produce outputs, but whose reasoning can be explained, justified, and challenged. It enables explainability and auditability by making knowledge dynamic, structured, traceable, and accountable, and it opens the door to a future of human–AI symbiosis, where machines serve as partners in reasoning rather than engines of imitation, and not as replacements for human judgment or creativity, but as collaborators in amplifying and extending both.

Bridging philosophy, mathematics, cognitive science, and computer science, *Logic Before Language* offers:

- A historical and epistemological critique of AI's drift from logic to statistical mimicry.
- A reconstruction of intelligence grounded in causal reasoning, structure, and explanation.
- A practical, future-focused framework for building AI systems that reason deductively, inductively, and abductively, generating auditable and justified conclusions, meaningful explanations, and new knowledge.
- A roadmap for trustworthy, transparent, and symbiotic machine intelligence.

For technologists, researchers, academics, policymakers, philosophers, deep thinkers, and AI enthusiasts who sense that something fundamental is missing in today's AI revolution, this book delivers both diagnosis and blueprint. It argues that the next era of AI will not be defined by bigger models or more data, but by a return to logic, meaning, and real understanding.

This is the case for AI that thinks and reasons. Not just one that talks.

## Security, Audit and Leadership Series

*Series Editor: Dan Swanson Dan Swanson and Associates, Ltd., Winnipeg, Manitoba, Canada.*

The scope and mandate for internal audit continue to evolve each year, as does the complexity of the business environment and speed of the changing risk landscape in which it must operate. The fundamental goal of this exciting series is to produce leading-edge books on critical subjects facing security and audit executives and practitioners. Key topics addressed include Leadership, Cybersecurity, Security Leadership, Privacy, Strategic Risk Management, Auditing IT, Audit Management and Leadership, and Operational Auditing.

*Modern Benford's Law: State of the Art Techniques for Audit and Compliance Professionals*
By Daniel J. McCarville

*Cumulative Effect: Cyber Security Guide for Directors and CEOs*
By Dr Vladas Leonas

*Digital Momentum: Building Real Change-Ready Enterprises*
By Brice Ominski

*Redefining Auditing in the Digital Era: Global Perspectives on Technology, Security, and Leadership*
Edited by Abdelmounim Bouziane

*Fire Brigades to Firewalls: A Public Safety Guide to Cybersecurity*
By John Kuforiji

*Bridging the Gap: Strengthening the Bond between Audit Committee and Internal Audit*
By Denise Cicchella

*CISO: Evolution of a Vocation Confessions of a Recovering CISO*
By Ron Baklarz

*Dark Faces in Cyber Places: Shattering Stereotypes and Leading with Legacy in Cybersecurity*
By Devon Bryan

*Logic Before Language: Rethinking AI in the Age of Illusion, Bertrand Russell and the Future of Real AI*
By Martin Milani

# Logic Before Language

## Rethinking AI in the Age of Illusion, Bertrand Russell and the Future of Real AI

Martin Milani

CRC Press
Taylor & Francis Group
Boca Raton London New York

CRC Press is an imprint of the
Taylor & Francis Group, an **informa** business

Designed cover image: Shutterstock ID: 1375479314

First edition published 2026
by CRC Press
2385 NW Executive Center Drive, Suite 320, Boca Raton FL 33431

and by CRC Press
4 Park Square, Milton Park, Abingdon, Oxon, OX14 4RN

*CRC Press is an imprint of Taylor & Francis Group, LLC*



ISBN: 9781041235668 (hbk)
ISBN: 9781041240808 (pbk)
ISBN: 9781003739999 (ebk)

DOI: 10.1201/9781003739999

Typeset in Caslon
by Deanta Global Publishing Services, Chennai, India

# Dedication

To my family, especially to my late father, who first introduced me to Bertrand Russell when I was a child. I still remember seeing the book in his hands, asking what it was, and listening as he tried to explain it to me. I tried reading it myself a few months later, probably far too young, and understood almost nothing, but it opened a door that never closed. To my late mother, whom I dearly miss; and to my wife Maryam and daughter Sophia, whose support made this book possible; and to all the brilliant engineers I have had the privilege of working with over the last two decades.

# Contents

# About the Author

**Martin Milani** is a technology entrepreneur, CEO, CTO, strategist, and systems architect whose work spans artificial intelligence, distributed systems, internet computing, and next-generation computing. Over the course of his career, he has built and led multiple technology companies, bringing advanced computing innovations from concept to large-scale commercial deployment.

Milani's work sits at the intersection of the boardroom and the laboratory. He is recognized for his contributions to cloud and edge computing, distributed systems, and large-scale intelligent platforms, tracing the evolution of computing from early UNIX-based systems to modern cloud architectures, microservices, and AI-driven infrastructures.

His current work focuses on the foundations of artificial intelligence, developing architectures that integrate perceptual learning, Bayesian inference, symbolic reasoning, fuzzy logic, and epistemic systems to explore how AI can move beyond statistical prediction toward systems capable of structured reasoning, real understanding, and verifiable conclusions.

Milani holds a B.S. in Computer Science with a minor in Mathematics from the University of Pittsburgh.

# Preface

We are living through the most convincing impersonation of intelligence the world has ever seen, hyped, celebrated, and deeply misunderstood. But what we are witnessing is not intelligence emerging; it is intelligence being performed. A statistical linguistic mask, not a cognitive engine.

This book begins with a confrontation: language is not intelligence. It never has been.

Machines now write essays, pass tests, generate code, and hold conversations in natural language. They appear to know everything and say it better than most humans can. But this fluency is an illusion. What they have mastered is not thought or intelligence; it is the *performance* of thought, and parroting words, it is not intelligence, but it plays one on your screen. And yet we trust them to summarize, explain, and decide. Why? Because they speak well. And in a world trained to mistake fluency for understanding, performance becomes proof.

Fluency doesn't just mislead; it blinds. It convinces us that comprehension has occurred when no true reasoning ever took place.

Today's AI systems offer answers without ancestry. They provide conclusions without ever showing how those conclusions were made. There is no real chain of reasoning to inspect, no structure to interrogate, no justification to evaluate. And a system we cannot question is a system we cannot trust.

This is not merely a technical gap. It is an epistemic one.

If intelligence is the capacity to understand, then understanding requires *visibility*: the ability to retrace an inference, test an assumption, and expose a contradiction. Without this, an AI can appear authoritative while being fundamentally ungrounded.

Auditability, traceability, and explainability are not optional features of intelligence; they are its foundation. When a model's internal process is inaccessible, the user is forced to accept its output on faith. Faith is not intelligence. And it is certainly not science.

At the heart of modern AI lies a profound confusion: the belief that sounding intelligent is the same as being intelligent. That language is not just the *expression* of understanding, but understanding itself.

Language is evocative, emotional, and culturally rich—but it is also ambiguous, imprecise, and easily manipulated. Intelligence, if it is to be trusted, requires more than patterns and predictions. It requires *reasoning*, the ability to represent knowledge, interrogate assumptions, resolve contradictions, and infer new truths.

Long before machine learning or neural networks entered popular imagination, the question of intelligence was understood as a question of structure. Not statistical performance. Not mimicry. Structure.

Bertrand Russell spent his life arguing that knowledge must be traceable, built from clear premises, connected by valid inference, and anchored in logical necessity. Clarity was not an aesthetic virtue for him; it was an epistemic one. A statement was not meaningful unless the reasoning behind it could be made explicit.

John McCarthy approached AI with the same conviction. Intelligence, he argued, required machines that could represent beliefs, reason about them, revise them, and justify them. Not merely react to input, but explain their output. Not just produce answers, but demonstrate how those answers followed from rules, facts, or assumptions.

The early AI pioneers did not see language as intelligence; they saw language as *interface*. Intelligence lived deeper—in the ability to construct, manipulate, and audit the structure of thought itself. Symbolic reasoning wasn't a limitation of early AI; it was its philosophical core, and it is the foundation this book seeks to reclaim.

Today's systems have inverted that hierarchy. They place language at the center and reasoning at the periphery. This book argues that the inversion must be undone, because intelligence begins not in expression, but in explanation.

Over time, however, the field drifted. Not because researchers abandoned logic, but because the world overwhelmed the tools we had. Symbolic systems were brittle, hard to scale with the limited computing power and hardware available at the time, and unable to absorb the messy irregularities of real-world data. We traded inference for interpolation. We replaced explicit structure with statistical approximation. We built systems that could summarize patterns but not understand them; that could generate language but not reason about the claims that language contained.

This shift did not begin as a philosophical rejection—it began as an engineering shortcut. But shortcuts have consequences. In the pursuit of scalability, we surrendered traceability. In the pursuit of fluency, we abandoned explainability. And in the pursuit of prediction, we forgot the essential requirement of intelligence: grounding in truth.

Today's dominant AI systems inherit that drift. They produce output without justification, confidence without comprehension, and coherence without causality. Their results look impressive, right up until the moment we ask why.

The intellectual lineage is clear but reclaiming it requires more than nostalgia. It requires a re-examination of what intelligence actually is, how LLM-based AI fails, and how real intelligence must be rebuilt.

The chapters ahead in this book argue that we must move beyond the seduction of fluency and return to the structure of thought itself. They chart a path from statistical mimicry to symbolic reasoning, from prediction to explanation, from parroting to partnership.

At the core of this journey is the idea of *Real Intelligence*—not purely artificial, not performative, but rooted in logic, grounded in truth, and capable of co-creating knowledge with us. Intelligence that is not just fast or fluent, but *structured, collaborative, and self-aware.*

What we need now is not bigger models, but a return to the fundamental requirement of any trustworthy intelligence: causal reasoning, generalization, deduction, induction, abduction, and the ability to show its work. Real understanding, in humans or machines, is not the act of generating the right sentence. It is the ability to reveal the structure beneath the sentence: the facts relied upon, the assumptions tested, the inferences drawn, and the alternatives rejected.

Without visibility into how a conclusion is formed, there is no basis for trust.

Without structure, there is no reasoning.

Without causal reasoning, there is no intelligence, only performance.

The future of AI will not be secured by scale alone. What is needed is not nostalgia for symbolic AI, and not a rejection of modern machine learning, but a synthesis: a layered cognitive architecture that restores reasoning, causality, auditability, and epistemic integrity to artificial intelligence.

Such an architecture would do what current LLM-based systems cannot:

- Maintain a traceable chain of inference.
- Explain why an answer holds.
- Reveal contradictions rather than obscure them.
- Invite inspection, correction, and verification.

It would replace the statistical opacity of today's models with a transparent structure of thought. It would not imitate intelligence; it would construct it. It would reason in real time, under uncertainty, with explicit causal grounding—not by predicting the next word, but by understanding the world those words attempt to describe.

In a world flooded with fluent but unexamined output, this direction offers something radically different:

Not more language, but more logic.
Not more data, but more causal and real understanding.

This book is not anti-AI. It is pro-*real* AI.

It asks: What would AI look like if we built it not to echo us, but to reason with us?

And it answers: by returning to logic before language, and intelligence before mimicry and illusion.

# Acknowledgments

This book grew out of decades of deep thought, work, conversations, failures, experiments, and arguments with people whom I have been fortunate enough to call mentors, bosses, colleagues, friends, and collaborators.

Many of the ideas here did not arrive fully formed; they were forged over years of building distributed and intelligent systems and platforms using advanced computational methods, dynamic constraint satisfaction, distributed reasoning, and real-time decision architectures that integrated Bayesian forecasting, symbolic constraints and rules, decision trees, and agent-based models with techniques such as Bayesian inference and fuzzy logic.

The core of these ideas first took shape during an AI course taught by Dr George Novacky at the University of Pittsburgh a long time ago, in a galaxy far away.

I am especially grateful to those who were willing to entertain questions that did not yet have names and who pursued solutions that had no clear path. Some of the systems we built were ahead of their time. A few did not end well, but most succeeded—some after minimal iteration, and others only after painfully long periods of iteration. Each of these experiences shaped my understanding of intelligence, complexity, and the structure of knowledge.

I want to offer special thanks to my mentor, John Seely Brown, who, as Director of Xerox PARC, cultivated the environment in which so many ideas that later shaped my thinking were explored, developed, and set into motion; and to the late Bill Coleman, founding CEO of BEA Systems, whose mentorship and leadership influenced my work and career. I also owe a great debt to the engineers, researchers, and technologists who were willing to challenge assumptions, debate architecture, and push back when ideas sounded too comfortable. I learned early that progress rarely comes from agreement; it comes from friction, contradiction, and the collision between theory and reality.

I would also like to thank the people who supported this project not just intellectually, but practically, by reading drafts, offering critique, and providing honest feedback. Their patience, skepticism, and encouragement helped refine ideas that began rough and unfinished into something that could finally be shared.

I am grateful to Dr Ludmila Morozova-Buss, who dared me to write this book; to the reviewers Dr John Seely Brown, Dr Warren Powell, Dr Shapour Vali, Dr Omid Ziaee (one of my brightest engineers); and to my dear friend and IP counselor, Mr Babak Kusha.

Any errors, blind spots, or oversights that remain are entirely my own. The insights, however, are the result of countless people who were curious enough to ask difficult questions and generous enough to explore possible answers.

# AI Assistance Statement

The author confirms that Artificial Intelligence tools were used for editorial refinement during the drafting and revision of this manuscript. All core ideas, arguments, philosophical content, research, reasoning frameworks (including the Real-Time Reasoning architecture), and original writing are entirely the intellectual work of the author.

AI tools were used only for grammar correction, punctuation, clarity improvements, rephrasing, readability checks, and paragraph-level flow refinement. No conceptual, analytical, or structural content was generated by AI. These tools were applied throughout the manuscript during the drafting and revision process.

Tools used:

- OpenAI ChatGPT (GPT-4 and GPT-5 series)
- Google Gemini (2025 versions)
- Microsoft Word Copilot (Microsoft Word version 2510)

All AI-assisted suggestions were reviewed, rewritten, and fully integrated by the author. The tools did not generate original material, did not contribute to argument formation, and did not produce thesis statements or conceptual elements for this manuscript.

# Introduction

Artificial intelligence was not meant to be a performance. It was meant to be a pursuit of understanding. From its earliest days, AI began with a philosophical question disguised as a technical one: can a machine represent knowledge, reason from it, and generate new truths that were not explicitly programmed? The fact that this question has been replaced by a far narrower one—can a machine predict the next word in a sequence—is one of the great inversions of our time.

Today we stand at a fork in the road, a consequential and dangerous one. We can continue building black-box systems that correlate without understanding, that remix training data without representing the world it describes, and that generate outputs without any capacity to explain, justify, or revise them. These systems operate only within the smooth interior of the bell curve, brittle at the boundaries where reality becomes volatile, nonlinear, and uncertain. Or we can build systems that model the world rather than the words about the world, systems that can reason causally, generate new knowledge, and navigate the long tails of uncertainty where meaningful outcomes often reside. Systems that do not merely induct from data, but that can deduct, abduct, and account for why conclusions should hold.

The deeper issue beneath this fork is not simply computational, but epistemological. Modern AI does not distinguish between truth and plausibility, between justified belief and fluent performance. It generates answers without representing the conditions under which those answers are true, without the ability to explain how they were derived, and without any internal mechanism for evaluating whether they should be believed. A system that cannot explain itself cannot be audited. A system that cannot be audited cannot be trusted. Bertrand Russell understood that reasoning is not merely a method for reaching conclusions, but a discipline for establishing justified truth, for connecting statements to evidence and inference. If we are to build machines worthy of trust, we must build systems that make their reasoning visible, their beliefs interrogable, and their conclusions grounded in structures that can be challenged, corrected, and improved. In a world where machines increasingly shape decisions with profound consequences, epistemic integrity is not a luxury; it is a requirement.

Human cognition is not powerful because it can detect patterns; it is powerful because it can represent knowledge, reason about causality, evaluate alternatives, contemplate counterfactuals, and construct new ideas that are consistent with what is already known. Intelligence is not a single capability, but a structure, layered and recursive, that binds perception, inference, explanation, and learning into a coherent system.

The modern AI revolution has achieved astonishing results in perceptual learning. Machines now speak, translate, recognize faces, and generate prose with fluency and confidence that would have been unthinkable just a decade ago. Yet fluency often conceals a deeper problem. When a system generates an answer based on statistics rather than understanding, without representing the conditions under which that answer is true, it cannot explain and justify its answer. When it cannot explain itself, it cannot be corrected. Without the ability to justify or revise its own reasoning, it cannot improve in any principled way. It performs intelligence rather than exhibiting it.

This book is a response to that tension. It argues that intelligence cannot emerge from surface-level prediction of language alone. It requires structure, meaning, and the ability to distinguish truth from plausibility. It requires systems that do not just produce statistical outputs, but that can show how those outputs follow from what they know and believe. This is a philosophical claim, but it is also a practical one.

If machines are to operate in scientific, medical, legal, financial, or civic domains, they must be able to reason, not merely guess.

Real-Time Reasoning (RTR) is a proposal for how this might be done. It is not a single algorithm or model, but a cognitive architecture built to integrate perceptual learning, probabilistic reasoning, symbolic logic, and explicit explanation. RTR is designed to make reasoning explicit rather than implicit, traceable rather than opaque, and collaborative rather than adversarial. Its goal is not to replace human thought, but to augment it by providing a system that can think with us in real time.

The ideas in these pages did not arise in a laboratory or a library alone. They were shaped by the experience of working with brilliant engineers who pushed back when abstractions collided with reality, of debating architectures that sounded elegant but failed in implementation, and of learning that progress often comes less from answers than from better questions. Many of the concepts in this book began as problems that refused to be solved.

My hope is not that the reader will agree with every argument in this book, but that they will consider a possibility that has been overshadowed in the rush toward bigger models and larger datasets: that intelligence, artificial or otherwise, begins not with prediction, but with reason. And that building machines capable of reasoning may require us to recover ideas that were present at the birth of AI, before we lost sight of them.

# 1

# The Illusion of Intelligence

We live in an age where machines talk, write, and answer our questions with uncanny fluency. They finish our sentences, draft our emails, summarize research papers, and even compose poetry. In the public imagination, they are brilliant, perhaps even intelligent.

But what does it mean to be intelligent?

Modern AI, dominated by large language models (LLMs), thrives on illusion. It mimics intelligence by mastering patterns in language, statistical echoes of human speech, scraped and stitched together into seamless responses. It sounds smart because it has read everything. But reading is not reasoning. Parroting is not understanding.

Language is seductive because it attempts to mirror thought while concealing its absence, flattening something dimensional into a shadow of itself. A well-formed sentence can feel like a conclusion, even when it carries no reasoning within it. Modern AI has perfected this illusion. The more eloquent the response, the more we mistake coherence for comprehension.

Yet intelligence is not defined by coherence; it is defined by justification. True understanding requires that every statement carry a traceable lineage, a path back to the premises and inferences that produced it. In philosophy, this is the heart of epistemology: knowledge must be justified, true, and explainable. Machines that cannot expose and explain how a conclusion was reached may simulate insight, but they cannot be trusted as sources of accuracy and truth. Intelligence without explainability and traceability becomes rhetoric without reason, noise without signal.

We begin with a confrontation: language is not intelligence. It never has been.

Language is expressive, beautiful, and infinitely powerful, but it is also ambiguous, culturally bound, and structurally imprecise. It

DOI: 10.1201/9781003739999-1

evolved not to express truth, but to share emotion, signal intention, and build connection. Language is not a tool of logic; it is a vehicle for communication and meaning. Meaning, as every philosopher from Aristotle to Russell has taught us, must be interrogated, not assumed.

Language did not begin as a structured system of thought. It emerged from grunts, gestures, and shared signals—tools for survival long before tools for truth. Early humans communicated danger, desire, and belonging through sound and rhythm, not logic or clarity. Over time, words formed from sounds, grammar from repetition, and eventually, whole symbolic systems evolved. But the evolution of language was not guided by rigor; it was negotiated. A shared compromise shaped by time, tribe, and context.

Language was constructed. Mathematics was not invented by humans; it was discovered. Its structures exist independently of us, embedded in the objective fabric of the universe, timeless, necessary, and indifferent to culture or lifeform. In a deeper sense, mathematics is the language of the universe itself.

Language absorbed metaphor, emotion, social cues, and ambiguity. It became a bridge for connection, not a scaffold for proof or truth. Precision came much later. Grammar itself was a retroactive invention, a structure imposed on something already fluid and alive. This tension between expressive language and precise thought became one of the central challenges of philosophy.

Few understood this more clearly than Bertrand Russell. To him, intelligence demanded clarity. Logic was the foundation. Ambiguous language obscured truth; symbolic reasoning revealed it. In *Principia Mathematica*, Russell and Whitehead tried to rebuild mathematics from pure logic—not because they were obsessed with formalism, but because they believed that real knowledge required structure. Truth was not what sounded right. It was what could be proven.

Today's language-based AI systems do not prove; they predict. They are statistical engines, trained to guess the most likely next word. That guess is shaped not by truth, but by frequency. The result is an astonishing mimicry of human communication. But it is not thought. It is not grounded in logic. It is not intelligence.

In this chapter, we will examine how the rise of language-first AI has confused fluency with reasoning—and why that confusion poses real dangers. We will unpack the architecture of modern LLMs and explore what they can (and cannot) do. We will trace the philosophical lineage of language and logic, revisiting Russell's warnings about the slipperiness of words.

And finally, we will begin to articulate a different vision, one rooted not in statistical pattern-matching, but in deduction, causality, symbolic abstraction, and real-time reasoning. A vision where AI is not a talking parrot, but a thinking partner.

This is not just a critique of today's AI. It is a call to return to intelligence before illusion. To logic before language.

## 1.1 Prediction Engines: How LLMs Actually Work

At their core, large language models are probability machines. They are trained on massive datasets of human textbooks, websites, articles, chats—and from that ocean of language, they learn one thing: what tends to come next.

Given a sequence of words, an LLM calculates the statistical likelihood of the next word, or fragment of a word, using a function called *softmax*, a probabilistic ranking of possible outputs. The model does not understand the meaning of the sentence. It recognizes that after "peanut butter and," the word "jelly" is more probable than "astrophysics." That's not understanding. It's pattern recall.

These models operate through neural networks, millions or billions of virtual "nodes" connected in weighted layers, shaped by training data and gradient descent. But despite the complexity, the objective is simple: predict what's next. It is a vast autocomplete engine, stretched to human scale.

And it works beautifully, at least on the surface. LLMs can write essays, answer questions, translate languages, and even imitate style. But beneath that surface is a void: no concept of truth, no model of the world, no internal logic. It does not know what it is saying. It only knows that what it says sounds right.

## 1.2 The Seduction of Fluency

Why do so many people mistake these systems for intelligence? Because fluency is persuasive.

Language is deeply emotional. We associate eloquence with insight, articulation with intelligence, confidence with competence. When an LLM speaks with clarity and style, we reflexively attribute understanding—even when none exists.

The distinction is subtle but existential. Reason introduces constraints—a demand that each claim survive interrogation. Language, by contrast, rewards persuasion. A reasoning system must be auditable: its conclusions reproducible, its logic inspectable, its path transparent and explainable. Without these properties, we cannot separate the plausible from the true, nor can we trust the system. The appearance of thought replaces the discipline of thinking.

This cognitive bias has been well documented. Humans are wired to anthropomorphize, projecting intent, awareness, even morality onto things that exhibit human-like behavior. If a chatbot tells a joke or apologizes when it's wrong, we don't just see code—we see personality.

And when the language sounds polished, we often skip the question of whether the content is valid.

This kind of illusion isn't new. In the 2002 Steven Spielberg film *Catch Me If You Can*, based on the true story of Frank Abagnale (portrayed by Leonardo DiCaprio), a young con artist convincingly impersonates a doctor—despite knowing nothing about medicine, simply by parroting confident language and tone. It was a con built on fluency. Today's language models do something similar. They talk like experts, echoing what they've seen before, projecting competence through tone and timing. But like Abagnale, they don't actually understand what they're saying.

But fluency is not fact. Style is not substance. And predictive eloquence, however impressive, is still just that, statistical prediction.

This illusion becomes dangerous when we put these systems in charge of consequential decisions: diagnosing illness, advising on legal matters, influencing public opinion, or summarizing complex issues. A model that doesn't know what it knows cannot reason about what it doesn't. It cannot check its logic, explain its conclusions, or know when it's wrong.

We risk replacing thinking with sounding right.

Explainability, then, is not a feature of intelligence—it is its essence. A mind, human or artificial, that cannot show its reasoning cannot claim understanding. The capacity to trace how conclusions arise is what allows knowledge to be tested, corrected, and trusted. This will become the central demand of all future architectures: that intelligence must not only *speak*, but *account* for its speech—that the path from *thought* to *word* be transparent, traceable, and true.

Without a visible, auditable, logical, and causally grounded chain of reasoning—an actual ancestry of inference, not a simulated "chain of thought" in which the output of one statistical sampling becomes the input to the next, allowing LLMs to mimic reasoning without ever performing it—there is no epistemic grounding. A model's output may appear correct, but without justification, it cannot be trusted as knowledge.

If explainability, epistemology, and trust are the essence of intelligence, how did we end up celebrating systems that cannot explain themselves? The answer is historical as much as technical: over decades, AI drifted from structure to surface—from rules and reasons to blind correlations, mimicry, and eloquence. The path to language-first AI was paved with noise, good intentions, and real ingenuity—but also with quiet flaws, compromises, and the absence of any epistemic signal.

# 2
# The Rise of Language-Based AI

The silver tongue of our modern machines did not appear overnight. It has been a long journey through which artificial intelligence gradually shifted its focus toward language. In the previous chapter, we saw how we can be captivated by an AI's fluency, the effortless flow of words that sounds so human. Now we ask: *How did we reach a point where fluent language became the primary measure of intelligence in AI?* The story of this transformation is one of both technological ingenuity and conceptual compromise, a path that has led us to equate linguistic eloquence with thought itself.

## 2.1 From Logic to Language: Early Visions and Setbacks

In the early days of AI, researchers believed that true intelligence would start with logic and reasoning. After all, human language is grounded in our understanding of the world; words have meaning because we connect them to ideas and facts. It made sense to these pioneers that a machine would need to *think* correctly before it could *speak* coherently. This view was shared by philosophers like Bertrand Russell, who insisted on clarity and truth in language. Russell worried about how ordinary language, with all its ambiguities, could mislead us. He even dreamed of a logically perfect language, one where every word had a precise meaning and nothing false could hide behind clever phrasing. Early AI researchers took a similar stance: teach the machine the rules of logic, give it a base of true information, and *then* natural language understanding would follow. At the same time, linguists like Noam Chomsky were pioneering formal grammatical theories, emphasizing that language had an innate, rule-governed structure—further reinforcing the idea that language could be

 DOI: 10.1201/9781003739999-2

understood through deep, symbolic analysis rather than surface-level patterns.

For a time, AI efforts reflected this logic-first approach. In the 1960s and 70s, projects like SHRDLU (a computer program that could manipulate virtual blocks and respond to commands in plain English) showed the promise of combining language with explicit reasoning. SHRDLU operated in a tiny, simple world of geometric shapes, yet within that world it understood descriptions, answered questions, and followed instructions. It did so by translating the English sentences into a structured, logical form, a kind of inner voice of reasoning. Around the same time, other systems tried to encode human knowledge in formal rules and ontologies (structured representations of concepts and relationships) so that a computer could reason about, say, a story or a conversation. There was an underlying faith that if we just captured enough rules of grammar and enough facts about the world, machine intelligence could master language in a meaningful way.

These early systems, though limited, were inherently auditable. Every conclusion could be traced back through explicit rules and representations. Their logic could be inspected, questioned, audited, and refined—a quality that modern AI, in its pursuit of fluency, has largely abandoned. They offered not just output, but explainability.

These early forays were illuminating, but they were also labor-intensive and brittle. Outside the carefully controlled scenarios (like SHRDLU's toy world), language kept breaking the machine's fragile logic. Anyone who has ever tried to pin down the "rules" for something as subtle as a joke or as context-dependent as a metaphor can imagine the challenge. By the late 1970s, it became clear that this approach, writing down every rule and fact a machine needed, was not scaling up. A famous setback in this era was the failure of machine translation projects. Researchers had optimistically predicted in the 1950s that computers would soon flawlessly translate Russian to English by following grammatical rules and dictionaries. Decades later, they were still nowhere near that goal. In 1966, a report to the US government bluntly declared these efforts a disappointment, leading to a major cut in funding. The dream of a perfectly logical language machine seemed to be running up against too much complexity.

## 2.2 The Statistical Turn: Data over Reasoning

Necessity, however, is the mother of invention. Faced with the limitations of rule-based intelligence, AI researchers tried a radically different tack in the 1980s and 90s. Instead of painstakingly teaching machines *how* to understand language, why not let them *learn* language by example? Rather than starting with logic, this approach would start with data, lots and lots of data. If you give a computer millions of sentences and documents, perhaps it can figure out patterns on its own. This was the beginning of the statistical revolution in AI, and it changed the trajectory of language-based AI forever.

This new approach treated language as a sea of probabilities rather than a tidy logical structure. Imagine you're writing a sentence: after the words "The cat sat on the," there's a good chance the next word will be "mat." How do we know that? Because in countless bits of English text, whenever "The cat sat on the" appears, "mat" often follows. Early language models were built on this insight. They learned from text by counting how often words follow one another. By the 1990s, these models could take a phrase and predict likely next words. Feed them enough literature, and they start finishing your sentences in surprisingly reasonable ways.

Notably, during this period, some researchers pursued a different kind of statistical reasoning—Bayesian inference, where probability was used not just to predict patterns, but to represent belief, model causality, and update conclusions based on new information. This thread, while often overshadowed by the rise of deep learning, maintained a closer affinity with structured logic and remains foundational to how intelligent systems can reason under uncertainty.

One watershed moment came when IBM researchers applied this idea to translation. Instead of teaching the machine what every word means, they fed it a huge bilingual text (Canadian parliamentary proceedings in English and French) and let it crunch the numbers. The result was a system that could translate simple sentences from French to English by statistically matching patterns of words—no deep understanding required. To many traditional linguists and AI experts, this was astonishing (and a bit disconcerting). The system didn't *know* French or English in any human sense; it couldn't explain what a word meant or whether a sentence was true. It was essentially performing a massive pattern-matching game, yet it worked better than many logic-based attempts. This success marked a turning point. Statistical methods started to outperform carefully handcrafted rules on more and more language tasks like speech recognition, spelling correction, and even grammar checking.

As this statistical approach gained ground, conceptual trade-offs were quietly being made. AI was, in effect, trading understanding for usability. Instead of trying to genuinely understand language the way a person does, the field settled for *approximating* language. The systems would be judged by how fluent and useful their outputs were, not by whether they truly reasoned about the meaning. It was a pragmatic bargain: you sacrifice the elegant certainty of logic, but you gain robustness and coverage. After all, a human linguist might craft a hundred rules and still miss the nuance of an idiom, whereas a statistical machine that has seen a billion sentences might get the idiom right simply because it has encountered something similar before.

Yet this pragmatic turn came at a cost. The reasoning trail that once allowed humans to audit, verify, and challenge a systems' conclusions was replaced by opaque correlations. The very act of understanding why an output emerged became nearly impossible. Trust in such systems shifted from epistemic comprehension to blind faith in training data.

So, data triumphed over explicit reasoning, and the old dream of encoding all knowledge in logical form faded into the background.

## 2.3 Prediction Machines: Fluency without Understanding

By the early 2000s, prediction had become the name of the game. Natural language processing systems were now essentially giant prediction engines. They took whatever text you gave them and tried to predict the most likely continuation or the most likely interpretation. If you've used a smartphone keyboard that suggests the next word in your text message, you've seen a simple example of this. But on a much larger scale, researchers were building far more powerful predictors. Thanks to the internet, an unfathomable amount of text, billions upon billions of words, was available to train AI models. This marked a fundamental turning point—from language as symbolic reasoning to language as statistical prediction. And thanks to faster computers and clever algorithms, these models could be made ever more complex.

The rise of deep learning pushed this trend into overdrive. Deep learning refers to using multi-layered neural networks (somewhat inspired by the brain's networks) that can automatically discover patterns in data. When applied to language, deep learning allowed AI to pick up subtler patterns than ever before. Instead of just counting word sequences, a neural network could learn abstract notions of syntax and context; for instance, it might infer that "cat" and "mat" have a relationship even if it never saw the exact sentence "the cat sat on the mat." By the mid-2010s, innovations in neural network design enabled models to handle long sentences and even paragraphs fluidly, keeping track of context better than earlier approaches.

All these advances led to the creation of Large Language Models (LLMs), the behemoths of modern language-based AI. An LLM is fed enormous swaths of text, from books, articles, websites, you name it—and it trains itself to predict missing words or the next sentence. Through this training, it effectively absorbs a vast amount of human writing style, facts, opinions, stories, and more (along with plenty of errors and biases). The result? Give it a prompt and it can generate a continuation that sounds uncannily like something a human might write. It can answer questions, produce a sonnet, or pen an essay on Bertrand Russell's philosophy with equal apparent ease. The key word here is "apparent." The LLM doesn't truly *know* Russell's ideas or *understand* poetry or history; it has simply learned how sequences of words tend to look when humans talk about those topics. It's performing an incredibly sophisticated autocomplete, one that draws on a huge memory of how language is used.

By turning language into a prediction problem, AI developers achieved a long-sought fluency. The machine no longer spits out garbled, robotic phrases; now it can produce paragraphs of text that read smoothly, even persuasively. In fact, the output is often so fluent that one forgets a machine is even speaking. This achievement has utterly dominated the public perception of AI in recent years. When people hear "AI" today, many immediately think of the conversational agents, the chatbots that can carry on a conversation or answer any question. The era of language-based AI has arrived in full, and with it comes a tendency to celebrate these systems as a kind of artificial mind that finally *gets it*.

Yet in chasing fluent language, the AI field largely abandoned the earlier quest for explicit reasoning. The new systems don't try to build a coherent model of the world or ensure that what they say is true—they simply try to sound right. They are trained to mimic the form of human communication, not to engage in the content of human thought. This is a profound shift. The old symbolic AI programs were like painfully honest students: they wouldn't say anything unless they could back it up with a rule or a fact they had been given (which meant they often stayed silent or sounded awkward). Today's large language models are like confident improvisers: they'll always have something to say, based on whatever patterns they've absorbed, but they have no reliable way to check if what they say makes sense in the real world. We gained a tongue and lost some of the mind behind it.

In gaining that tongue, we also lost logical reasoning and its traceability. When reasoning is replaced by statistical inference, accountability and auditability dissolve. A system that cannot explain its steps cannot be audited; a model that cannot epistemically justify its claims cannot be trusted. We built machines that sound right, even when they cannot show why they are right. We replaced reason with sweet talk.

### 2.4 Eloquence as a False Idol of Intelligence

This evolution raises a critical question: Have we been mistaking the appearance of intelligence for intelligence itself? It's tempting to equate eloquence with thought. If something talks like a brilliant person, we feel it must *be* intelligent. This temptation isn't new. In 1950, Alan Turing famously proposed that if a machine could hold a conversation indistinguishable from a humans', we'd have to call it intelligent. He imagined a text-based Q&A, an "imitation game," where a judge wouldn't be able to tell if answers were coming from a person or a computer. Decades later, we've built machines that arguably pass this test; they can chatter away and often you'd be hard-pressed to know there's no person behind the screen.

But the Turing Test, and our own intuitions, can be misleading. Fluency in language is one facet of intelligence, one that is very easy for us to notice. We humans are so tuned to language that we tend to judge a mind by its words. We often assume someone who speaks eloquently is intelligent and someone who struggles with words is not, even though we know (if we reflect) that this isn't a foolproof measure. We've all heard politicians or pundits who sound confident and articulate while saying very little of substance. Conversely, a person might be wise and knowledgeable yet not very articulate. In AI, this bias in our perception becomes even more problematic. We have created entities that excel at the outward performance of language with none of the inward depth that language is meant to convey.

The result is a kind of *cognitive illusion*. When an AI writes a convincing paragraph or gives a confident answer, we may feel as if it must understand what it's talking about. We find ourselves using words like "think" or "know" to describe what the AI is doing. After all, if it answers a question about World War II in detail, doesn't it *know* history? If it can discuss the emotions of a character in a novel, doesn't it *understand* empathy? It is so easy to fall under the spell of fluent output and assume there's an intelligent mind behind it. Even experts sometimes get caught in this trap, momentarily treating the AI as if it were a clever student or colleague.

The danger here, as Russell would remind us, lies in ambiguity and deception—though not deception by malice, but deception by appearance. Russell was deeply concerned with how language can make false or meaningless statements seem meaningful. A grammatically correct sentence can still be nonsense or untrue; it can lull us into accepting an absurdity because it sounds properly phrased. Modern AI brings this old philosophical problem to life in a new way. A language model can say things that are precise-sounding, grammatically impeccable, and utterly wrong or empty of sense. For example, if asked a question it doesn't truly have information on, the model might simply fabricate an answer that *looks* right. It might cite studies that don't exist, or give a detailed explanation that it actually stitched together from unrelated bits of training data. The output is fluent *fiction*. Without any understanding of truth, the AI has no compass to distinguish fact from its own confident fictions.

This is why mistaking eloquence for reasoning is so problematic. When we treat a predictive text engine as a thinking being, we are essentially giving a free pass to whatever it says, as long as it sounds good. We might trust advice that has no basis, believe claims that haven't been vetted, or make decisions swayed by the smooth talk of a machine that has no stake in truth. The issue is not just hypothetical. There have already been instances of people getting incorrect medical or legal guidance from AI assistants because the output was fluent and authoritative sounding. It's as if we've summoned a brilliant orator who can speak on any topic but has no obligation to be correct. As Russell wryly pointed out, someone spouting nonsense with great confidence can even gain power or prestige despite being deluded. In our context, an AI's eloquence could lead us to give it more credit than it deserves if we aren't careful.

To borrow one of Russell's own metaphors: a philosophy that cares only about language and not about reality is like a boy who removes the pendulum from a clock so it will run faster. Yes, the hands spin more freely, but the clock no longer tells the time. With today's AI, we have a clock without a pendulum. The words pour out faster and more smoothly than ever, but we cannot be sure if they still track reality. The pendulum we removed was the grounding in logic and truth. What remains is a dazzling, but unmoored, flow of language.

## 2.5 Reconnecting Words with Truth

Understanding how we arrived at this point is the first step in addressing the challenges it poses. The rise of language-based AI has been a story of triumphs: we solved problems that once seemed impossible, and we gave machines a voice that can engage with us on our own linguistic turf. But it has also been a story of letting go of certain principles, like the strict adherence to logical reasoning and truth-checking. We have, in a sense, put the linguistic cart before the logical horse—celebrating a facsimile of intelligence that rolls along on data-driven momentum, even as the guiding rationality remains absent.

The next frontier is not just more data or larger models, but the restoration of *epistemic integrity,* the principle that every claim should carry an auditable trail of reasoning and justification.

True intelligence must be both *explainable* and *traceable*; its reasoning paths open to scrutiny, its claims auditable in principle. Only then can we rebuild trust between human and machine, grounding fluency once again in verifiable thought.

As we move forward, we must ask pressing philosophical questions: What *is* intelligence, if not just fluent conversation? Can a machine be said to "understand" anything if it lacks a firm grasp of truth and falsehood? Should we continue down this path of ever-greater fluency, or should we reintegrate the discipline of logic into AI's evolution? These questions urge us to look beyond the beguiling surface of language and seek the deeper structures of reasoning beneath. In the chapters ahead, we will explore these questions, examining why language alone, no matter how polished, cannot substitute for genuine understanding. We will consider how a balance might be struck, where the progress of language-based AI is not abandoned but is instead grounded once again in the very thing our early AI pioneers and philosophers like Russell held dear: a commitment to logic and truth.

Having witnessed the rise of language-based AI and its seductive power, we are now prepared to delve into the heart of the matter: the distinction between sounding intelligent and *being* intelligent. This journey will challenge us to rethink whether the mirror we have created, one that so convincingly reflects human-like speech, truly contains a mind behind it, or if it is a dazzling empty echo. The answers will shape not just the future of AI, but also our understanding of our own intelligence and the tools we build in its image.

# 3

# The Mirage of Meaning

What happens when fluency masks emptiness? When coherence is confused with comprehension?

That is the defining trap of language-based AI.

Large language models don't think; they complete. Their goal is not to arrive at truth but to simulate what truth might sound like. Every sentence they produce is the result of statistical next-word prediction based on an immense corpus of human writing. (As outlined in Chapter 1, "Prediction Engines," these systems optimize next-token likelihood rather than truth, a design that produces coherence without comprehension.)

The result can feel astonishingly coherent. But coherence is not cognition. It is the appearance of understanding, not its presence.

This is epistemic opacity at scale: systems that can reproduce the form of reasoning while concealing the absence of reason itself. They produce statements that can be verified syntactically but not semantically.

This is the mirage of meaning: the illusion that because a sentence makes sense, it must have been understood by the system that produced it. But LLMs do not know what their sentences refer to. They have no grounding in reality, no connection between symbol and substance, between language and the world it describes.

They do not know that Paris is a city, or that gravity pulls objects down, or that two contradictory statements cannot both be true. They generate words that seem to align with these facts, but they do so blindly. Their knowledge is implicit, not explicit. And when it breaks, it does so silently, confidently asserting falsehoods with the same style and tone as truth.

We call these hallucinations. But they are not hallucinations in the human sense: false perceptions within a conscious framework. They

DOI: 10.1201/9781003739999-3

are statistical anomalies, unmoored from meaning, yet often indistinguishable from truth.

Fluency becomes most dangerous when we mistake confident language for competent judgment. A system built only to statistically predict the next word cannot examine its own claims, question its premises, or detect when it has wandered into fabrication. It cannot distinguish uncertainty from error or signal when its internal model has broken down. Yet when its output arrives wrapped in polished prose, we instinctively grant it authority. The result is a subtle but profound hazard: a mechanism with no grasp of truth presented in the form most likely to be believed, statistical correlation masquerading as comprehension.

It may sound like it understands, but it doesn't. And if we confuse prediction with comprehension, we risk replacing understanding with mimicry.

### 3.1 Coherence without Comprehension

How can a system that doesn't think produce such coherent language?

The answer lies in the statistical machinery that drives every large language model. These models work by assigning probabilities to sequences of tokens: fragments of words, punctuation marks, or entire words depending on the language model's granularity. When given a prompt, they generate a response by selecting the most likely next token, then the next, and so on, until a complete sentence, or paragraph, emerges.

This process is powered by mechanisms like the softmax function, which converts raw output scores (logits) into probabilities. Behind the scenes, the model is navigating a space of 50,000+ potential tokens at each step, computing which sequence best fits the prompt based on patterns learned from massive training corpora.

To understand what this actually means, consider the mechanics behind that prediction step.

When people say LLMs "predict the next word," it's not quite that simple. What they're actually doing is choosing from a fixed vocabulary of about 50,000 tokens, not just full words, but common fragments like *re-*, *-tion*, or *-ology*, plus punctuation marks, spaces, symbols, and even emojis. These tokens are derived using algorithms like Byte Pair Encoding or SentencePiece, which break down language into statistically common building blocks. During training, the model is fed a massive diet of language, hundreds of thousands of books, millions of websites, Wikipedia articles, social media posts, and more. It learns to break that ocean of text into tokens, then predict them one at a time.

At each step, the model scans this entire list of 50,000 tokens and assigns a probability to each one, based on everything it has seen so far. These probabilities are calculated from internal scores, called *logits*, which are passed through a function known as softmax. Softmax turns those raw scores into a ranked probability distribution: essentially, a weighted guess. The model doesn't pick the next word because it understands the sentence; it picks the token that is statistically most likely to come next. This is purely statistical probability, not semantics, comprehension, or understanding.

In this process, uncertainty is compressed into probability, but probability without ontology or model of reference. What emerges is not a model of the world, but a model of words about the world. Each layer refines its guesses by statistical proximity, not by logical coherence or causal truth. The result is an epistemic flattening: meaning reduced to frequency, reasoning reduced to recurrence. We can measure accuracy, but not understanding; optimize likelihood, but not truth.

You can picture it like a massive probability tree, or a 50,000-slot roulette wheel, where each slot represents a token and the wheel is tilted based on what came before. During training, the model adjusts its predictions by comparing them to the actual next token in the training data. The mismatch is measured using a concept called Kullback–Leibler (KL) divergence, a way of quantifying how far off its guess was from the truth. Over time, the model learns to tilt the wheel more accurately. But what it's optimizing is *frequency*, not *meaning*. It becomes astonishingly fluent, not because it understands, but because it has seen millions of similar sequences and learned to echo them with statistical precision.

One of the key metrics guiding this process is Kullback–Leibler divergence (KL divergence), a statistical measure of how one probability distribution diverges from a reference distribution. During training, LLMs are optimized to minimize KL divergence between their predictions and the actual token distributions found in human text.

But here's the catch: minimizing KL divergence doesn't mean understanding. It means aligning guesses with historical frequencies. It's the difference between statistical forecasting and true comprehension and reasoning. It creates a mirror, not a mind, a probabilistic echo of prior language rather than a reasoning engine that knows what it's saying or why.

Beneath this fluency lies a deeper epistemic problem. When systems generate text by optimizing probability, they cannot distinguish between coherence and correctness, between parroting and understanding. The outputs are statistically justified, but not semantically verified. We can trace gradients, but not reasoning paths. We can visualize weights, but not thoughts.

In this sense, the opacity is not accidental; it is architectural. The system's very design buries cause beneath correlation. Meaning becomes emergent rather than explicit, and truth becomes whatever pattern best minimizes loss. Without structure, we cannot audit or interpret; we can only observe. These are systems that perform understanding without possessing it, fluent in the language of reason but silent on its logic.

In the next section, we'll look more closely at how this statistical mimicry, while astonishingly effective at sounding intelligent, still lacks any internal concept of truth, logic, or causal coherence.

### 3.2 The Need for Structure

What LLMs reveal, unintentionally, is how good we've become at mimicking meaning without understanding it.

They shine at fluency, but they fail at grounding. They master patterns, but miss purpose. And when pressed beyond their training distribution, they hallucinate, not because they are flawed, but because they were never built to know.

If we want real intelligence, machine cognition that reasons, explains, and understands, we need a new foundation. Not one based on the frequency of words, but on the structure of thought.

This requires a return to logic. To systems that represent knowledge explicitly, reason through contradictions, and trace how conclusions follow from premises.

Structure is not merely a technical preference; it is the architecture of epistemic integrity. Without it, truth cannot be traced, reasoning cannot be inspected, and knowledge cannot be trusted.

In science, structure is the audit trail of understanding: equations in physics, proofs in mathematics, protocols in software, all ways of exposing how conclusions follow from premises. It is what allows one mind to reproduce, challenge, or refine the reasoning of another.

Language-based AI lacks this scaffolding. Its outputs cannot be decomposed into logical steps or epistemic commitments; its reasoning, if we can call it that, leaves no trail to follow. What we gain in fluency, we lose in inspectability.

To move forward, we must restore this architecture, systems whose inferences are explicit, whose conclusions can be interrogated, and whose logic can be revised. Only then can intelligence, human or artificial, regain its trustworthiness.

Bertrand Russell warned that natural language, while rich and expressive, is too imprecise to serve as the foundation of knowledge. He advocated instead for symbolic logic, a language of structure, where ambiguity gives way to clarity, and assumptions must be stated, not implied.

If we want AI that can move beyond parroting human speech, if we want thinking and reasoning machines that understand logic, not talking ones, then we must rebuild from this foundation. We must move from illusion to inference.

While Russell's work laid the foundation for logical formalism, it was John McCarthy, decades later, who carried that torch into artificial intelligence. McCarthy's vision for AI wasn't built on mimicking language or behavior but on encoding knowledge through logic, rules, and inference engines. This lineage, from Russell's symbolic rigor to McCarthy's declarative logic and his AI programming language LISP, formed the philosophical backbone of early AI.

*LISP*, short for "LISt Processing," was the programming language McCarthy created to express symbolic reasoning in code. Unlike procedural or numerical languages, LISP was designed specifically to manipulate symbols and recursive structures, making it ideally suited for building intelligent systems that could reason and learn. Before neural networks took center stage, AI was envisioned as a reasoning machine, not a statistical one.

McCarthy believed that intelligence, human or artificial, must rest on the ability to represent the world symbolically and draw conclusions through structured inference. He proposed that thinking could be formalized in a way that was both machine-readable and semantically rich, just as Russell had sought to formalize mathematics in *Principia Mathematica*. Among McCarthy's contributions was the Situation Calculus, a logical framework for representing and reasoning about dynamic worlds, how actions lead to new situations, and how those situations affect what an agent knows or can do. He also introduced non-monotonic reasoning, a form of logic that allows systems to revise or withdraw conclusions when new information emerges, much like how humans change their minds in light of new facts. These were not mere programming constructs; they were attempts to mirror human-like flexibility and logical depth.

In this sense, McCarthy did for machine intelligence what Russell had done for epistemology and mathematics: he transformed logic from an abstract discipline into a tool for real-world understanding. His legacy isn't just LISP or early AI experiments; it's the enduring idea that true intelligence must be explainable, modular, and logically sound. While today's AI is largely driven by data and probability, McCarthy's lineage reminds us that reasoning, and not reaction, is the highest form of machine cognition. And in this lineage, we find the intellectual bridge that connects Aristotle to Russell to real AI.

In the next chapter, we return to Russell's original critique of language and revisit the intellectual roots of this problem: the sloppiness of speech.

# 4

# The Sloppiness of Speech

Language is beautiful. It seduces. It connects. It gives voice to love, war, poetry, and politics. But it was not designed for clarity. It was not born from a desire to reason, but from the need to communicate and to relate.

And therein lies the danger, especially in an age where machines mimic our speech without understanding our thoughts. Language's greatest strength, its flexibility, becomes its most perilous flaw when confused with truth.

Its flexibility erodes traceability: words shift meaning without leaving a reasoning trail, making claims sound true without being auditable.

Language was never designed to be logical.

It emerged to express emotion, signal needs, and build connection. It evolved organically, layered with culture, metaphor, ambiguity, and contradiction. Its power lies in its flexibility. But that same flexibility makes it unreliable when precision matters.

Few understood this better than Bertrand Russell.

To Russell, natural language was dangerously imprecise. It allowed people to say things that sounded meaningful but collapsed under scrutiny. In his seminal essay *On Denoting* (1905), he introduced the Theory of Descriptions, an attempt to resolve linguistic confusion through logic. His goal wasn't to make speech clearer; it was to replace it with symbolic structure that could not lie, mislead, or obscure by accident.

Russell gave the example: "The present king of France is bald." It seems grammatically correct, but there is no current king of France. Is the sentence true? False? Meaningless? Russell argued that the sentence was structurally flawed. To fix it, you must reframe it in logical terms: "There exists an x such that x is the present king of France, and x is bald." Since no such x exists, the entire proposition is false, not

DOI: 10.1201/9781003739999-4

meaningless but logically resolvable as false. And if a sentence this simple can hide structural confusion, imagine what happens when we train machines on billions of them.

Each sentence in that corpus becomes an unverified assumption. When aggregated, they form systems that can generate answers, but not justify them. Explainability dies in the noise.

This was the essence of Russell's critique: that language must be stripped of ambiguity and rewritten in logical form to be properly understood. That sentences which appear clear are often hiding layers of contradiction, assumption, or nonsense.

For Russell, imprecise language was not just an academic issue; it was a philosophical crisis. He believed that sloppy phrasing allowed entire schools of thought to flourish on shaky foundations. If you couldn't say something clearly, he suspected, perhaps you weren't thinking clearly either.

His student Ludwig Wittgenstein would later carry this obsession further, arguing in the *Tractatus* that the limits of language were the limits of thought itself. If logic was the bedrock of meaning, then anything outside of logic was, quite literally, nonsense.

This problem persists not just in philosophy, but in AI.

Large language models make the same mistake: they treat linguistic form as semantic fact. They cannot audit their own conclusions because their reasoning chain is statistical, not logical. Their outputs are fluent but non-traceable because no causal or symbolic path links input to conclusion, only opaque probability weights and echoes of correlation without cause.

They assume that what sounds true must be true. But, like the sentence about France's imaginary monarch, the structure often hides a void.

Consider these common examples of ambiguity:

- "Visiting relatives can be annoying." (Who's visiting whom?)
- "He saw the man with the telescope." (Who had the telescope?)
- "I didn't say she stole the money." (Seven meanings depending on emphasis.)

These sentences demonstrate how meaning can shift based entirely on context, tone, or implied relationships. Humans resolve these ambiguities using common sense, situational awareness, or intent. But language models lack these faculties. They rely on pattern frequency, not actual knowledge of the world.

Without a causal model or verifiable reference frame, every answer is a guess disguised as comprehension, a sentence put together based on probabilistic weights with no epistemic audit trail.

Real-world consequences of linguistic sloppiness are everywhere.

In popular culture, the book *Eats, Shoots & Leaves* highlights how punctuation ambiguity can radically alter meaning. In legal history, a contract missing a single comma once cost a Canadian company over $1 million when a dispute over contract termination hinged on whether a clause was interpreted as restrictive or additive.

In diplomacy, the 1956 Suez Crisis partly unfolded due to misinterpretations of international statements, where vague assurances were mistaken for binding guarantees. After Egyptian President Gamal Abdel Nasser nationalized the Suez Canal, Britain, France, and Israel launched a coordinated military intervention. The United States, the Soviet Union, and other nations condemned the attack, but much of the crisis stemmed from earlier diplomatic communications where intentions had been expressed in deliberately ambiguous language. Britain, for instance, interpreted certain US and UN statements as tacit approval for action; in reality, no such approval existed.

The result was a catastrophic misreading of diplomatic "permission"—leading to international humiliation, accelerated decolonization, and a permanent shift in global power dynamics. Ambiguous phrasing, intentional or accidental, helped trigger one of the most consequential geopolitical miscalculations of the 20th century.

Literature and religion offer even starker examples.

Sacred texts like the Bible have been interpreted in radically contradictory ways over centuries, sometimes promoting compassion, sometimes justifying violence, because metaphor and ambiguity leave wide gaps for human projection. The same verses have been invoked to support abolition and to justify slavery; to preach pacifism and to sanctify war; to promote charity and to defend accumulation.

Part of this arises from the nature of metaphor itself: metaphors help illuminate abstract ideas, but they also distort them. They trade clarity for connection, precision for emotion.

Without a structured logical framework for interpretation, readers fill in gaps based on culture, desire, and bias, seeing not what is written, but what they want to find. Sacred language, like all fluid language, becomes less a map and more a mirror. And when the stakes are moral, social, or existential, that ambiguity can shape centuries of conflict.

As Bertrand Russell warned, when precision is sacrificed for poetry, meaning becomes unstable, and truth becomes a matter of interpretation, not proof.

As Kurt Gödel showed, truth must exist independently of metaphor and interpretation.

Metaphors drift; structures endure.

And when meaning drifts, so does judgment, and so does civilization.

What fails here is epistemic integrity, the ability to connect claim to cause, language to logic, and statement to truth.

These examples reveal a core truth: when stakes are high, ambiguity isn't charming; it's dangerous. Language must be structured, not just evocative.

And today, as we build AI models that generate language without understanding, we risk repeating the same ancient mistake at machine speed.

Fluency without structure is not intelligence; it is an invitation to drift. And when the world listens to machines that speak without understanding, civilization once again stands on unstable ground.

Recent examples show how this ambiguity leads not just to confusion, but to real harm. LLMs have generated summaries of legal cases that never existed, complete with fabricated citations. In medicine, AI has recommended contraindicated drugs due to misinterpreting symptoms phrased in ambiguous ways. One bot told a suicidal user to "go ahead" after misreading the context of a mental health query.

These are not edge cases. They are the product of a system that recognizes shape and sound, but not meaning. That treats grammar as truth. That confuses "this sentence appears in many trusted places" with "this sentence is true."

Even humans struggle with meaning when language is sloppy. We lean heavily on intuition, inference, and context. But AI lacks even that. It operates without grounding, making fluency dangerous.

Natural language is like a beautiful but unstable bridge, elegant, suggestive, but full of cracks if walked on too firmly. Logic is steel scaffolding. It's not warm, but it holds. In a world where AI must do more than entertain, we need steel, not smoke.

The results can be consequential. In real-world applications, LLMs have misinterpreted medical queries, generated false citations, or recommended unsafe actions, all because they modeled phrasing, not understanding. In legal tech, bots have produced plausible but fabricated case law. In journalism, LLMs have hallucinated sources, eroding trust.

What's needed isn't just better training data but a different approach entirely. One rooted in structure.

Russell's legacy shaped more than philosophy. His work underpins fields like description logic, semantic web, and knowledge representation in AI. His insistence on clarity over comfort lives on in systems that demand explicitness, where truth is computed, not inferred by vibe.

The urge to replace the sloppiness of speech with formal systems didn't stop with Russell. Gödel would go on to show the limits of these systems, but the effort itself seeded entire disciplines. Formal logic, model theory, and description logics emerged from the same impulse: to say only what could be proved, and to reject anything that couldn't be meaningfully expressed in structure.

In short: if you want machines to reason, you must first teach them what reasoning requires. Not fluency. Not frequency. But structure.

And structure begins by rejecting the sloppiness of speech.

If we want AI to reason, it must understand not just how to sound right, but how to *be* right. That requires rejecting the fuzziness of speech in favor of something stricter. Something traceable. Something true.

Structure restores auditability. Logic re-establishes explainability. Mathematics offers traceability to truth.

Only when meaning can be followed step by step can it be trusted.

In the next chapter, we begin building that structure, starting with the language of logic itself: mathematics. Because LLMs inherit not only our eloquence, but also our imprecision. Their fluency is trained on our sloppiness. When AI stumbles, we shouldn't just blame the models. It's the foundation that's unstable. Their fluency mimics our flaws. If we want reasoning machines, we must give them a different substrate—something logic can stand on.

# 5

# Mathematics as Meaning

## 5.1 Why Logic Matters More than Language

The power of logic didn't begin with computers. It began with clarity, an ancient pursuit of truth untangled from emotion, ambiguity, and assumption. While language evolved to express human emotion and need, logic was invented to understand complex constructs and test human claims. And few grasped this divide more profoundly than Bertrand Russell.

Russell believed that mathematics, rightly understood, was not just a tool for calculating. It was the highest form of reasoning, a symbolic architecture where clarity ruled and truth could be proven. He wasn't alone. He stood at the summit of a long tradition that saw logic as the true substrate of intelligence.

Mathematics did more than codify truth; it made reasoning auditable. Each step could be examined, replicated, and justified. Where language persuades, mathematics demonstrates.

> Mathematics, rightly viewed, possesses not only truth, but supreme beauty… because it is the most exact expression of thought.
>
> — **Bertrand Russell**

## 5.2 The Lineage of Logic

Long before Bertrand Russell, the foundations of logic were laid by thinkers who saw reason as the path to truth.

Aristotle was the first to formalize this intuition. In the 4th century BCE, he introduced *syllogistic logic*, a system of deductive reasoning built around structured propositions. If all men are mortal, and Socrates is a man, then Socrates is mortal. It sounds simple today, but


DOI: 10.1201/9781003739999-5

Aristotle's insight was revolutionary: truth could follow from form. Logic wasn't just a way to think; it was a method to know.

Euclid, writing a century later, took that idea from philosophy into mathematics. His *Elements* wasn't just a geometry textbook; it was a blueprint for structured knowledge. Every theorem flowed from axioms through deductive steps. It showed that even space itself could be reasoned about using logic. Euclid turned geometry into a system, a self-consistent world built from first principles.

Fast forward to the Enlightenment, and we find thinkers like René Descartes, who sought to ground knowledge in certainty. "Cogito, ergo sum"—I think, therefore I am—was not just a slogan, but an attempt to build truth from indubitable premises. Leibniz, meanwhile, dreamed of a *universal calculus*, a symbolic system that could express all human thought. If disputes could be reduced to logic, he believed, "it would suffice to say: Let us calculate."

These were not just abstract dreams. They were visions of intelligence—of knowledge purified from confusion, argument, and ambiguity.

But it was Bertrand Russell who would bring this lineage into the modern age. He didn't just admire these thinkers; he sought to complete their project.

Russell believed that logic was not merely a philosophical tool. It was the bedrock of knowledge itself. And in the early 20th century, together with Alfred North Whitehead, he set out to prove it, literally.

### 5.3 Logicism and the Foundations of Knowledge

At the height of his intellectual mission, Russell partnered with Alfred North Whitehead to write *Principia Mathematica*, a monumental work that sought to rebuild all of mathematics on a foundation of pure logic.

Their ambition was audacious: to show that every mathematical truth, from basic arithmetic to complex theorems, could be derived from a small set of logical axioms using a precise system of formal rules. No appeals to intuition. No reliance on common sense. Just symbols, definitions, and rigor.

And nowhere is this more famously demonstrated than in their attempt to prove **1 + 1 = 2.**

What most people consider self-evident took Russell and Whitehead hundreds of pages to formally derive. On page 362 of Volume I, after layers of definitions and logical scaffolding, they finally arrive at:

> From this it will follow that 1 + 1 = 2.

In *Principia Mathematica*, numbers are not primitive notions. Even "1" must be constructed using logical building blocks. The number 1 is defined as the class of all unit classes, i.e., sets that contain exactly one element. The number 2 is the class of all two-membered sets. Addition becomes a logical operation on these abstract classes.

So to prove that 1 + 1 = 2, Russell and Whitehead first define what 1 means, what + means, and what 2 means, without using any of those concepts informally. Then they demonstrate, through symbolic manipulation, that the logical structure of combining two singleton sets results in a set that belongs to the class we have defined as "2."

The full symbolic proof is daunting, filled with notation like $\vdash$, $\wedge$, and $\varepsilon$ but the message is clear: even the simplest mathematical fact requires deep structure if we want certainty.

Russell was not doing this to be difficult. He was doing it to be precise. In a world awash with assumptions, he wanted to know that truth could be traced, not just intuited.

That traceability is what separates logic from belief. In logic, every conclusion carries a lineage, a visible chain of inference linking premise to proof. This is the original blueprint of explainability: a reasoning process that can be inspected, challenged, and verified.

This is the intellectual backdrop for logicism: the belief that mathematics is reducible to logic, and that true intelligence must be built on this kind of foundation.

And that belief still matters, especially in an era where AI systems routinely conflate correlation with causation, and eloquence with understanding.

### 5.4 Contrast with Natural Language

If logic is about structure, precision, and provability, natural language is the opposite: flexible, emotive, and deeply ambiguous.

Bertrand Russell recognized this tension early. To him, the problem with natural language wasn't just that it was vague; it was that it allowed us to believe we were being precise when we weren't. People confuse grammar with logic. They hear clarity in a sentence's rhythm, not in its structure. And this illusion of clarity can mask profound confusion.

In *Principia Mathematica*, Russell and Whitehead built a formal system where every term had a defined role, every rule had a reason, and no step could be skipped. You couldn't say something was true—you had to prove it. But in natural language, we often say things that sound meaningful but collapse under scrutiny. Words shift meaning depending on context. Sentences carry unspoken assumptions. And logical fallacies slip through dressed in fluent syntax.

Consider the difference between these two statements:

- "All bachelors are unmarried men."
- "Time heals all wounds."

The first is tautological, logically true by definition. The second is poetic, metaphorical, and context-dependent. Language allows both to be expressed with equal fluency. But only one of them survives a logical test.

This is what makes natural language so powerful, and so dangerous for AI.

Human beings evolved to communicate socially, not logically. We're experts at reading tone, inferring context, and filling in gaps. When we say, "It's cold in here," we often mean, "Please close the window." That kind of inference comes naturally to us, but it requires layers of cultural, emotional, and situational knowledge.

Machines, on the other hand, treat language literally, or statistically. When they process a sentence, they rely on surface form, not structured meaning. They don't know that "cold" is a temperature, or that a closed window might change it. They don't know what "here" refers to. They don't know what we *meant*. They only know what's been *said*, and what's statistically likely to come next.

This is where symbolic logic shines. It doesn't guess. It defines. It requires that every variable, every function, and every relationship be spelled out. There is no hidden context. No implied meaning. Nothing is assumed. Everything is constructed from first principles.

Russell believed this was essential, not just for mathematics, but for any system that claims to represent truth. He once wrote:

> Wherever possible, substitute constructions out of known entities for inferences to unknown entities.

That is: don't assume; define. Don't infer; construct. Don't hope the listener understands; make it impossible to misunderstand.

Natural language evolved to communicate *between minds that already share a model of the world*. Symbolic logic was built to describe *the world itself*, independent of the minds describing it.

And this distinction is critical for AI. Because if we want AI to do more than parrot human language, if we want it to reason, to explain, to act, we cannot rely on a system built to emote. We need one built to know.

### 5.5 Universality and Culture-Free Intelligence

If natural language is bound to culture, context, and convention, then mathematics, at its core, is culture-free.

A child in Japan, a physicist in France, or an alien intelligence on the other side of the galaxy might all recognize the truth of the Pythagorean theorem. Not because they share a language, but because the structure of the theorem maps to reality in a way that transcends expression. Math describes relationships that are not negotiated; they are discovered.

Russell believed this was no accident. Logic and mathematics, he argued, represent the most precise, and most universal, forms of thought. They do not require a shared culture, vocabulary, or tradition to be understood. They are portable architectures of reasoning.

In *Principia Mathematica*, Russell wrote:

> Pure mathematics consists entirely of assertions to the effect that if such and such a proposition is true of anything, then such and such another proposition is true of that thing. It is essential not to discuss whether the first proposition is really true, and not to mention what the anything is, of which it is supposed to be true.

In other words, math is not about the world; it is about the structure of the world and the truth itself.

That's what makes it the ideal substrate for intelligence.

Human cognition evolved in a messy environment, filled with half-truths and emotional inference. Language evolved to survive that messiness, to create cohesion, not precision. But if we want machines to reason about facts, test hypotheses, and understand the world beyond human stories, we must build them on systems that don't rely on shared assumptions.

This is where symbolic reasoning shines. In logic, you must define your terms. You must trace your steps. And the conclusions you reach are only as valid as the axioms you begin with. It's not a game of words; it's a game of structure.

This is the promise of logicism: that the deepest truths about numbers, about structure, and about causality are independent of how we talk about them. They are what remain when the poetry is stripped away and only the skeleton of thought remains.

Russell once wrote:

> "If logic gives us no knowledge of the external world, it gives us the skeleton of all knowledge."

That skeleton, bare, abstract, precise, is the only foundation on which truly intelligent systems can be built. Without it, AI systems will continue to impress us with fluency but fail us when asked to reason.

### 5.6 The Role of Incompleteness

Just as Russell and Whitehead were constructing a fortress of logic around mathematics, a quiet revolution was forming in the mind of a young Austrian prodigy: Kurt Gödel.

In 1931, Gödel published his *Incompleteness Theorems*, shaking the very foundations of formalism. His core insight was both brilliant and unsettling: any sufficiently powerful formal system capable of expressing arithmetic will contain true statements that cannot be proven within the system itself.

For Russell, this was both intellectually humbling and deeply troubling. *Principia Mathematica* had been built on the dream that logic could contain and prove all mathematical truths. Gödel showed that dream was, in a sense, incomplete—not because logic failed, but because completeness itself was an illusion. But for the next generation, this wasn't an ending; it was a starting point. Alan Turing asked a new kind of question: not what is true, but what is computable.

Gödel's work didn't refute logicism; it reframed it. It revealed that even in a perfect system, there are boundaries. That truth may sometimes extend beyond proof. And that no machine of pure deduction could ever fully account for the universe of mathematical meaning.

Russell respected Gödel's brilliance, even as it unsettled the foundations he had spent his life building. But rather than undermine the value of logic, Gödel's theorems elevated it by showing that logic was not omnipotent, but honest. It could define what it knew, and by implication, what it could not.

This idea is critical to the design of intelligent systems. A truly reasoning AI must not only deduce truth but also know when it cannot. It must recognize the limits of its own axioms, the assumptions that underlie its conclusions, and the boundaries of what its system can express.

That humility, formalized by Gödel, is the next step in intelligence: not just reason, but self-aware reasoning. Not just logic, but metalogic. The ability to reason about reasoning, to inspect the structure of belief and know where the light fades into shadow.

### 5.7 What AI Forgot

For decades, AI was born from this foundation. The early pioneers, John McCarthy, Marvin Minsky, Allen Newell, and Herbert Simon, were deeply influenced by logic, mathematics, and the formalist tradition. AI was not supposed to sound smart. It was supposed to think.

McCarthy, the father of AI and creator of the LISP programming language, envisioned machines that could reason symbolically. He believed that intelligence meant understanding context, drawing inferences, and making decisions based on explicitly modeled knowledge, not just reacting to patterns. For McCarthy, reasoning also had to be explainable. A machine should be able to articulate why it reached a conclusion, trace its steps, and justify its choices. Without the ability to explain its own reasoning, he believed, a system was not thinking at all.

But somewhere along the way, that vision was lost.

As the field pivoted toward statistical machine learning, then deep learning, and now LLMs, the emphasis shifted. Instead of building systems that reasoned, we built systems that mimicked. Instead of modeling knowledge, we harvested text. Instead of asking what was true, we asked what was likely.

The irony is profound: the very models that now dominate AI, transformers, LLMs, neural networks, are still powered by math. KL divergence, backpropagation, stochastic gradient descent, vector spaces, and probabilistic modeling are all mathematical constructs and symbolic without which LLMs would not work at all. The computation may be nonlinear, but the bedrock is logic and structure.

Yet these systems apply that math to language, not logic. To correlation, not causation. They treat language as a dataset, not a puzzle. They do not model the world; they model how humans talk about the world.

Russell would find this inversion bizarre. McCarthy would likely find it tragic.

What AI forgot is not the math. It's the meaning.

And the path forward isn't to abandon language, it's to reintroduce structure beneath it. To recover the lineage of symbolic reasoning, Bayesian inference, and structured deduction that once defined the field.

Because if we want AI to do more than talk, if we want it to think, we must return to logic as the substrate, not the afterthought.

### 5.8 Why This Still Matters

Russell's work wasn't just a philosophical exercise; it was a map to clarity in a world increasingly ruled by noise. His logicism was not about making mathematics cold or mechanical; it was about making reasoning precise, traceable, and universally communicable.

Today, that clarity is more urgent than ever.

In a world of algorithmic persuasion, deepfakes, language models, and viral misinformation, we no longer suffer from a lack of expression; we suffer from a surplus of it. We don't need machines that can talk more; we need machines that can reason better.

This is why Russell's legacy matters, not just for mathematicians or philosophers, but for the future of AI. If we want systems that can *understand*, rather than simply *respond*—that can *explain*, rather than merely *generate*—then we must return to logic as the foundation.

Mathematics, in Russell's vision, was the most exact expression of thought because it made truth demonstrable. That same clarity, structured, symbolic, and causal, must now become the north star for artificial intelligence.

Because if we want AI to act as more than a mirror of human language, we must first teach it how to think.

Explainability, traceability, and epistemic integrity are not modern inventions; they are mathematical virtues.

And long before computing machines existed, one man had already written the blueprint for that thinking.

### *5.8.1 George Boole and the Mathematics of Thought*

George Boole, the English mathematician, philosopher, and logician, did not merely study mathematics; he redefined what it meant to think.

Before Boole, logic was a branch of philosophy; after him, it became a branch of mathematics. In his 1854 masterpiece *An Investigation of the Laws of Thought*, Boole proposed something extraordinary: that reasoning itself could be expressed through symbols and equations. Thought, he argued, obeyed laws, and those laws could be represented mathematically.

Boole fused three disciplines that had rarely touched: mathematics, philosophy, and logic. In doing so, he created the first formal system capable of representing reasoning independent of language. His insight was both elegant and revolutionary: every proposition is either true or false, and the relationships among truths can be expressed through simple operations—AND, OR, NOT. From this foundation, Boolean algebra was born.

What Aristotle had conceived in prose, Boole translated into formalism. He didn't describe logic; he *mechanized* it. His algebra transformed abstract reasoning into structure. It was the first genuine language of thought—one that could, in principle, be executed by a machine. And though no such machine existed in his lifetime, Boole had already written its logical framework and grammar.

Nearly a century later, Claude Shannon would take Boole's abstract equations and make them physical. In his 1937 master's thesis at MIT, Shannon demonstrated that electrical circuits of relays and switches could perform Boolean operations—that "True" and "False" could become "On" and "Off." Logic, once philosophical, became electrical. Boole's symbols had found their hardware. Shannon's work transformed reasoning into engineering and laid the foundation of the digital world.

Then Alan Turing gave that logic motion. His conception of the *universal machine* showed that symbolic operations could be carried out mechanically, that logic itself could be automated. Boole had defined the mathematics of thought; Turing proved it could think procedurally. Logic had become computation, and the very foundation of modern computing was operationalized.

Through Boole, Shannon, and Turing, logic evolved from abstraction to execution.

Boole gave it mathematical form.
Shannon gave it physical form.
Turing gave it procedural form.

Together, they created the foundation of modern computing and, by extension, artificial intelligence.

Every program, every algorithm, every circuit, every chip, and transistor still speaks Boole's language. Each executes trillions of logical decisions per second: AND, OR, NOT—the elemental grammar of thought. Even the most advanced neural networks, buried beneath layers of probabilistic modeling, depend on this same binary logic at their core. Logic is the substrate on which all computation rests.

And yet, somewhere along the way, we forgot.

Modern AI systems, powered by statistical learning and massive datasets, have drifted from this foundation. They operate *on* logic but not *within* it. They simulate reasoning without understanding its structure. They predict what might sound true rather than deducing what *is* true. They run on Boolean hardware yet disregard Boolean truth, and without Boolean mathematics of thought, none of what they do would be possible.

Boole's legacy reminds us that intelligence begins with logic, not language, not data, not probability.

Without logic, there is no computer science.
Without computer science, there is no AI.

Therefore, without logic, there is no AI.

Logic is not one discipline among many; it is the root from which all others grow. It is what makes truth computable, meaning transferable, and intelligence possible. Boole didn't just invent symbolic reasoning; he created the mathematics of thought, and in doing so, set humanity on the path toward machines that could think.

The story of Boole, Shannon, and Turing was not just about machines. It was about meaning—about the idea that the structure of thought could be mirrored in mathematics. What began as mathematical logic had once again converged with the philosophy of thought.

When logic became computation, and computation became digital, the next question emerged: How does logic handle the real world that is not purely binary?

### 5.9 Lotfi Zadeh and the Logic of Continuity

In the 1960s, another thinker, Lotfi Zadeh, working at UC Berkeley, realized that in the real, nonlinear world, between true and false lay an entire spectrum of truth. Where Gödel had revealed that even the most perfect logical system would contain truths it could not prove, and Russell had pursued precision through exclusion, Zadeh sought understanding through inclusion. He recognized that truth in the physical world is seldom absolute, that between certainty and contradiction there exist degrees of belief, confidence, and meaning that must themselves be understood and reasoned toward conclusive truth and epistemology. It was as if, by applying the right contrast filter to a grainy photograph, Zadeh showed how blurred or imprecise realities could resolve into sharper distinctions of foundational truth—how logic itself could bring clarity and epistemic decisiveness to shades of gray.

Zadeh called this framework fuzzy logic, a system built not to replace classical logic, but to extend it. Where Boolean reasoning divided the world into true and false, ones and zeros, fuzzy logic allowed values in between, partial truths that could be evaluated, compared, and resolved deterministically with mathematical precision. It didn't abandon determinism; it refined it. Instead of guessing, as probabilistic systems do, fuzzy logic quantified ambiguity and reasoned through it, assigning degrees of truth that could still lead to definitive and clear conclusions through reasoning.

This was a profound shift. It suggested that logic could operate within uncertainty without surrendering to the randomness of a probabilistic perspective—that reasoning could be continuous rather than discrete. Fuzzy logic was not stochastic; it was graded. It didn't ask, "What's likely?" It asked, "To what degree is this true?" In doing so, it bridged the rigid exactness of symbolic logic with the fluid complexity of the real world, providing a structured way to think in gray while still reasoning toward black or white.

In many ways, Zadeh's contribution closed a circle that had begun with Aristotle. Where Aristotle gave us the syllogism, Bertrand Russell the structure, and Gödel the humility of incompleteness, Zadeh offered the missing texture—the acknowledgment that truth, while logical, can also be continuous. Fuzzy logic turned the binary skeleton of thought into a living continuum of understanding. It extended binary algebra into the gray shades of the real world, and then resolved them back into binary clarity: true or false.

This, one imagines, must have put a huge smile on Bertrand Russell's face.

The continuum Zadeh revealed was more than mathematical; it was philosophically mathematical.

# 6
# Philosophia Mathematica

Most people think of mathematics as cold, abstract, or even detached from reality. But that couldn't be further from the truth. In fact, mathematics is arguably the most successful structure humans have ever discovered and formalized—not because it crunches numbers, but because it reveals the underlying structure of the world. Whether describing the curvature of spacetime or the logic behind software, mathematics offers something nothing else can: a precise mirror of how things must relate if they are to make sense at all.

Mathematics was never just about numbers. It was, and still is, the most exact language we have for expressing relationships, dependencies, structure, and truth. At its highest level, it becomes something else entirely: a philosophy of reality.

Russell believed this deeply. To him, mathematics was a logical art form. It was not a collection of techniques, but a mode of thought, one capable of revealing the structure of all knowledge. His 1919 book *Introduction to Mathematical Philosophy* attempted to bring these ideas to a broader audience, stripping away the dense notation of *Principia Mathematica* while preserving its core insight: that mathematics is built from logic, and logic is the foundation of reason.

> Pure mathematics is the class of all propositions of the form 'p implies q', where p and q are propositions containing variables, and the variables are unrestricted.
>
> **—Bertrand Russell**

This may seem abstract, but it's powerful. Russell's insight was that the heart of mathematics isn't numbers; it's implication. It's about how one truth necessarily follows from another. Replace numbers with logical relationships, and suddenly math becomes a language of structure, capable of modeling anything from ethics to algorithms.


DOI: 10.1201/9781003739999-6

Mathematics, in Russell's framing, was not about numbers, but about forms. It was about how things relate, how conclusions follow from assumptions, and how one can deduce structure from rules. It wasn't merely a tool for calculating outcomes, but a system for expressing what must be true.

This was radical for its time. It meant that the truths of mathematics were not discovered by passively observing the world; they were derived by reasoning about symbols. And that meant you could construct an entire universe of knowledge, starting from nothing but logic itself.

This is where mathematics and machine learning part ways. The latter relies on statistical correlation: what tends to be true, what usually follows. Mathematical logic, by contrast, is about necessity. It asks: What must be true if certain assumptions hold? That distinction, between high-probability and provable truth, is not just technical. It's foundational to how we define intelligence; it determines whether a system is predicting or reasoning.

Russell saw this as more than elegant. He saw it as necessary.

Natural language, in contrast, was unstructured. It relied on shared context, cultural assumptions, and intuitive interpretation. It was rife with synonyms, ambiguities, and emotionally loaded associations. Mathematics was its antidote: a form of expression where every term had a definition, and every conclusion had a proof.

Russell's project was ultimately a philosophical one: to rebuild knowledge on a foundation that did not shift. To replace the softness of speech with the sharpness of symbols. To give thinking itself a formal structure.

His influence extended far beyond philosophy. Thinkers like Rudolf Carnap and Willard Van Orman Quine carried Russell's commitment to clarity into the heart of 20th-century analytic philosophy. Alan Turing drew from Russell's formalism when imagining the limits of computation. And John McCarthy, the father of AI, saw logic not just as a tool, but as the essential scaffold for machine reasoning.

The impact of Russell's logicism helped birth fields like computer science, formal semantics, and logic programming. Languages like LISP and Prolog bear the imprint of this lineage. The dream was not simply to build machines that could compute; it was to build machines that could reason.

To understand why this mattered, consider a simple example of symbolic logic in action:

If it rains, the ground gets wet.

It rains.

Therefore, the ground is wet.

$$(\text{Formal: } P \rightarrow Q, P \vdash Q)$$

Symbolic reasoning forces precision. There's no room for ambiguity or assumption. Every step is traceable. This is the opposite of natural language, where even a clear sentence can be interpreted multiple ways depending on context.

You can extend this further.

All mammals breathe air. Whales are mammals. Therefore, whales breathe air.

$$(\text{Formal: } P \rightarrow Q, R \rightarrow P, \vdash R \rightarrow Q)$$

These kinds of chained inferences, so basic to human reasoning, are precisely what symbolic logic handles effortlessly, and what many AI systems today still struggle to do.

Mathematical logic, in a sense, is to thought what source code is to software: a structured syntax that makes intentions explicit and testable.

Where source code enforces consistency, logic enforces coherence—and coherence is the true measure of understanding.

It is in this spirit that we propose a new foundation for AI.

If intelligence is not just the ability to generate answers, but to reason, to infer, to deduce, and to understand the answers it gives, then AI must be rooted in a system of structure, not just a sea of statistics. It must echo Russell's vision: that logic is not just a tool of mathematics, but the very form of intelligence.

> Mathematics, rightly viewed, possesses not only truth, but supreme beauty... because it is the most exact expression of thought.
>
> **—Bertrand Russell**

> Development of Western science is based on two great achievements: the invention of the formal logical system (in Euclidean geometry) by

> the Greek philosophers, and the discovery of the possibility to find out causal relationships by systematic experiment (during the Renaissance).
>
> **—Albert Einstein**

The Greeks gave us formal systems. The Enlightenment period, spanning the Renaissance and the Scientific Revolution, gave us causality. Russell sought to unify both, to fuse logic with science, mathematics with metaphysics. In many ways, his work was a continuation of this grand tradition: not merely understanding the world as it is, but as it must be, if it is to be consistent.

Today, we live in a world overflowing with data, but lacking structure. In AI, we've prioritized surface-level fluency over deep reasoning. Russell reminds us that the goal is not to mimic answers, but to build systems that *understand* why an answer follows from a premise, and when it doesn't.

In the next chapter, we move from Russell's philosophical logic to the practical architectures of AI. We will ask: If logic is so central to intelligence, why did symbolic AI fade? What replaced it? And what might it look like to bring it back—not as nostalgia, but as necessity. Today's LLM-based AI doesn't lack data; it lacks structure. It lacks reasoning. It lacks explanation.

This is where we turn to real-time reasoning.

Mathematics, at its deepest level, is not just a language or a tool; it is the architecture of reason itself.

Yet the journey to fully understand, formalize, and extend structured reasoning was far from complete.

Across centuries, the invention of reason had to be discovered, forgotten, rediscovered, and finally reborn —

a long, fragile arc stretching from Socrates to the dawn of artificial intelligence.

It is to that longer, sweeping story that we now turn.

# 7
# Reason Had to Be Invented

Evolution gave us pattern recognition. It gave us the instincts needed to survive in a dangerous, unpredictable world. But it did not give us reason.

Our minds evolved to react, to associate, to link events by coincidence. True reasoning—the ability to uncover hidden causes, to interrogate assumptions, to build knowledge from firm foundations—was a conscious breakthrough. It was one of humanity's rarest and most fragile inventions, as precious as fire or mathematics.

Early humans did not reason logically. They were connectionists, mainly driven by perceptual learning. They survived by shallow and simple pattern matching, by correlating events that happened close together, related or unrelated, often without understanding cause and effect. Lightning struck—and rituals were invented to summon or banish it. Illness came—and amulets were worn. In this early world, shallow correlations were mistaken for deep causal structures, and intuition ruled over structured thought.

Life itself was uncertain, volatile, and dangerous. In a world where predators lurked, weather shifted without warning, and disease struck invisibly, survival often depended not on understanding why things happened, but on reacting swiftly to what seemed to happen. The mind, in those early days, became a repository of myths and rituals, a library of guesses stitched together by coincidence, fear, and hope. To mistake pattern for law and habit for truth was not a flaw; it was an evolutionary necessity.

But the invention of reason changed everything. It was not enough to see that things happen together. True intelligence demanded asking whether they must happen together, and why. It demanded separating chance from necessity, myth from structure, coincidence from causality.


DOI: 10.1201/9781003739999-7

And once discovered, reasoning did not remain safe. Across history, it has been born, extinguished, and reborn—carried forward only by those willing to defend it against the tides of superstition, authority, and complacency. Each rebirth came at great cost. Each collapse was a warning.

Today, as we stand at the dawn of building Artificial Intelligence, we face a new turning point. The danger is not just that reason may be forgotten, but that, in our rush to create machines that speak fluently and predict patterns, we may repeat the oldest error: building minds that correlate without understanding, that imitate without knowing, that confuse appearance with cause.

If we are to create true intelligence, artificial or otherwise, we must not abandon the fragile invention that made us intelligent in the first place: the discovery of causality, of reason, of structure behind the surface of things.

It is along this hard-fought, fragile path that we journey now, from Socrates to Turing, from the first steps of structured inquiry to the first dreams of reasoning machines.

## 7.1 Birth of Structured Thinking

For most of early civilization, knowledge was inherited, not created. Truth was handed down through myths, traditions, and sacred stories, a tapestry of memories stitched together more by authority than by proof. Questions were discouraged. Certainty was prized over inquiry.

Yet even amid this landscape of unquestioned truths, a crack began to appear. In a few extraordinary minds, the old way of accepting the world gave way to a radical instinct: to question it.

The first true revolution in thinking began not with answers, but with questions. And it began in Athens, in the 5th century BC, with a man named Socrates.

### *7.1.1 Socrates (470–399 BC): The Birth of Disciplined Questioning*

Socrates did not leave behind a system of logic, a theory of knowledge, or a written record of his thought. What he left behind was something even more powerful: a method.

In a world dominated by tradition and intuition, Socrates introduced a radical idea: that beliefs must be examined, not merely accepted. He taught by asking questions, probing assumptions, exposing contradictions. Through relentless dialogue, he showed that much of what people claimed to know was built on shaky foundations. It was not enough to inherit beliefs; one had to test them, challenge them, and see if they could survive the assault of reason.

Socrates' famous declaration, "The unexamined life is not worth living," captured the spirit of this intellectual revolution. Truth was not something to be received; it was something to be earned through questioning.

In dialogues like the *Euthyphro*, Socrates would pose deceptively simple questions, "Is something good because the gods love it, or do the gods love it because it is good?", and in doing so, unravel the contradictions hidden inside commonly accepted beliefs. Knowledge, he showed, required more than memorization. It required a ruthless search for coherence, for causes behind appearances.

This method, the disciplined questioning of assumptions, laid the groundwork for structured thinking itself. For the first time, knowledge was not a matter of authority or memory, but of logical coherence. Socrates shifted the focus from memorizing perceived or dictated assumptions and truths to interrogating them to understand them. It was the first great step toward intelligence based not on imitation, but on reason.

### *7.1.2 Plato (427–347 BC): The World of Forms and Abstract Structure*

Plato was a student of Socrates and the first great architect of philosophical systems. Where Socrates had focused on questioning everyday assumptions, Plato sought to build a deeper theory of reality itself. If human beliefs were so often flawed, he reasoned, then the world perceived through our senses must itself be an imperfect reflection of some deeper, more perfect reality.

This led Plato to propose one of the most influential ideas in the history of thought: the theory of Forms. Beneath the messy, shifting appearances of the physical world, he argued, exist eternal, unchanging "Forms" or "Ideas," perfect patterns that our everyday experiences only dimly imitate. Justice, beauty, equality, these were not just words or social agreements. They were real, independent structures, existing beyond the reach of time and decay.

In his famous *Allegory of the Cave*, Plato illustrated this vision vividly. He asked his listeners to imagine prisoners chained inside a cave, able to see only shadows cast on the wall by objects behind them. The prisoners mistake these shadows for reality because they have never seen the true objects that cast them. In the same way, Plato suggested, most people mistake sensory experience for truth, never realizing that true reality lies beyond what the senses can perceive.

In modern terms, Plato's method could be seen as an early form of abductive reasoning, the practice of inferring unseen structures from incomplete evidence. He taught that truth often lies not in what we see, but in what explains what we see. In this sense, Plato might even be considered a distant philosophical ancestor of Sherlock Holmes: deducing hidden realities behind confusing and fragmented appearances.

Plato's work laid the intellectual foundation for a crucial shift: the recognition that reality could be modeled—that hidden beneath appearances were structures that could be discovered, understood, and reasoned about. Knowledge was no longer simply the accumulation of observed facts; it was the disciplined pursuit of underlying forms, patterns, and principles. This move toward abstraction would become essential for everything that followed, from Aristotle's formal logic to Euclid's axiomatic systems, and ultimately to the logical underpinnings of artificial intelligence itself.

### *7.1.3 Aristotle (384–322 BC): Logic, Causality, and the Systematization of Reasoning*

Aristotle was a student of Plato, but he would soon chart a very different path. Where Plato had looked upward toward abstract, perfect Forms beyond the senses, Aristotle turned his gaze outward, into the world itself. He believed that reality was not a flawed copy of higher ideals, but something that could be directly studied, categorized, and understood through careful observation and reasoning.

Aristotle's greatest contribution to the birth of structured thinking was the formalization of logic itself. He developed the system of syllogisms, structured arguments where conclusions necessarily follow from premises. In Aristotle's framework, reasoning was no longer an art; it became a science, with rules and structures that could be studied and mastered. It was the first systematic attempt to map how truth could be derived step by step, from known facts to new knowledge.

Beyond logic, Aristotle placed causality at the center of his understanding of the world. He argued that to truly know something, it was not enough to describe its properties; one had to understand its causes, the reasons for its existence and behavior. He famously distinguished four types of causes: material, formal, efficient, and final. This deep focus on causes made Aristotle the first philosopher to treat the why of things as essential to knowledge—not just the what.

As a simple example of Aristotle's approach to logic, consider the classic syllogism:

All men are mortal.
Socrates is a man.
Therefore, Socrates is mortal.

Here, truth emerges not from intuition, tradition, or authority, but from structured reasoning—from the relationship between premises and conclusions.

Through his work, Aristotle transformed the pursuit of knowledge from a mystical or poetic endeavor into a disciplined method. Observation, categorization, causality, and deduction became the new pillars of understanding. In doing so, Aristotle built the first great intellectual engine for structured, logical thought, one that would echo through the Renaissance, the scientific revolution, and the foundations of modern computing.

Even today, the fingerprints of Aristotle's logic are everywhere.

Every software program—every artificial intelligence system based on decision trees, symbolic reasoning, or expert rules—owes its structure to Aristotelian principles.

Even programming languages, the very syntax by which we instruct machines, are built on logical frameworks: conditionals, operators, structured flows of reasoning encoded line by line.

When we write algorithms, when we program machines to make inferences, we are following a path that began with Aristotle's vision:

that knowledge could be made mechanical through the systematic application of reason.

### *7.1.4 Euclid (Circa 300 BC): The Architecture of Knowledge*

By the time Euclid lived and worked in Alexandria around 300 BC, the intellectual seeds planted by Socrates, Plato, and Aristotle had taken root. But it was Euclid who would perform one of the greatest acts of intellectual architecture in history: building an entire system of knowledge from first principles.

Euclid's *Elements* is often remembered as a book about geometry. In reality, it was something far greater, a revolution in how knowledge itself could be organized. Beginning with a small set of self-evident truths, or axioms, Euclid showed that one could logically derive an entire body of complex truths, theorem by theorem, each following inevitably from what came before. Knowledge, he proved, could be constructed like a building: one solid block resting securely atop another.

Where earlier thinkers had focused on the art of reasoning or the exploration of causes, Euclid brought rigor. His method was unforgiving. Every proposition had to be proved, every proof had to rest squarely on earlier ones, and every logical leap had to be justified. In doing so, Euclid gave birth to the axiomatic system, a framework that would shape mathematics for over two thousand years and become the blueprint for formal systems in science, logic, law, and computing.

The axiomatic method Euclid championed remains at the heart of modern disciplines ranging from theoretical physics to computer science and artificial intelligence—wherever vast structures are built from simple, well-defined foundations. When we design algorithms, construct formal proofs, program intelligent systems, or encode laws and legal precedents, we are echoing Euclid's vision: that rigorous structures can rise from basic, carefully constructed principles.

The spirit of Euclid is not confined to science and mathematics alone. Our entire legal and judicial systems—with their reliance on foundational principles, logical consistency, precedent, and structured argument—are profoundly Euclidean in their design. Wherever systems are built not by the accumulation of disconnected facts but by careful construction from basic rules—in law, in software, and in AI—the legacy of Euclid lives on.

In the lineage from Socrates' questioning, to Plato's abstraction, to Aristotle's systematization, Euclid was the first great builder, proving that human reason could not just probe and categorize the world, but construct entire worlds within the mind, governed by pure logic.

#### *7.1.5 From the Rise of Reason to Its Collapse*

For a moment in history, the trajectory seemed clear. From Socratic questioning to Platonic abstraction, from Aristotelian logic to Euclidean construction, humanity had laid the foundations of a world built not on superstition or authority, but on structure, causality, and proof. A framework for true intelligence, grounded in reason, had begun to emerge.

Yet history does not always move forward in a straight line.

The light of structured reasoning, so painstakingly kindled, would soon be dimmed. In the centuries that followed, logic and reason would be eclipsed by dogma, causality would give way to simple, shallow, poorly understood correlation and myth, and the architecture of reason would crumble under the weight of tradition, dogma, superstition, and fear—mainly fear of questioning and thinking freely and objectively.

It would not be the last time.

The collapse of reason in the ancient world holds a warning for us today, especially as we stand once again at the threshold of building new intelligences.

Before we can move forward, we must understand how, and why, humanity once lost its greatest invention.

### 7.2 Collapse into Darkness

The invention of structured reasoning had lifted humanity toward a new horizon: a world where truth could be tested, where knowledge could be built, and where causes could be uncovered behind appearances. Yet for all its promise, this fragile achievement was not inevitable, nor was it irreversible.

In the centuries following the fall of classical civilizations, the disciplined pursuit of logic and causality gave way to something far older, and far more dangerous. Superstition reclaimed its throne. Patterns were mistaken for causes, rituals for knowledge, and tradition for proof. Truth was no longer something to be discovered through inquiry; it was something to be received, recited, and obeyed without question, memorized rather than understood, repeated rather than reasoned.

Connectionist thinking—recognizing patterns without understanding causes—replaced structured, causal reasoning. Simple correlation supplanted true explanation. Humanity fell back into a mode of perceptual learning: the blind association of events, symbols, and rituals, without the deeper scaffolding of logic or proof. Knowledge became a mirror of appearances, not a ladder to deeper truths.

It was not merely a collapse; it was a return.

The human mind, which had once risen toward questioning, abstraction, and systematic logic, slipped backward into the ancient modes that had dominated before Socrates, before Plato, before Aristotle—a world where perceptions and appearance ruled over understanding, and tradition ruled over truth.

Fear of questioning replaced the courage to reason. Authority replaced investigation. Correlation, however shallow or coincidental, replaced causality. Humanity, once on the cusp of a structured and expanding understanding of the world, turned inward, back toward the comforting and imprisoning certainties of myth, decree, and intuition.

The architecture of reason had not merely been neglected; it had been buried, deliberately and deeply. And with it, the progress toward true intelligence, both human and, one day, artificial, was halted for centuries.

### *7.2.1 From Collapse to Reawakening*

For centuries, the architecture of reason lay buried beneath layers of fear, tradition, and unquestioned belief. Humanity survived, but it did not advance. The sciences stalled. Exploration turned inward. Knowledge became the memorization of decrees, not the discovery of causes.

Yet the spirit of inquiry, though smothered, was never entirely extinguished. In time, a few brave minds would once again dare to question the unquestionable. They would look not to tradition, but to nature itself. They would seek not just to memorize what was taught, but to understand what was real.

Slowly, painfully, a reawakening began.

The pursuit of structured, causal reasoning, so briefly glimpsed in the classical world, would return. And with it, humanity would once again step onto the long, perilous path toward true intelligence.

## 7.3 The Reawakening

The collapse of structured reasoning had plunged humanity into centuries of stagnation, but the human spirit, restless and irrepressible, could not be silenced forever. Slowly, haltingly, a few extraordinary minds began to rediscover what had been forgotten: that the world could be questioned, that reality could be understood not through superficial correlations and authority, but through careful observation and causal reasoning.

They turned their eyes outward, not toward tradition, but toward nature itself. And in doing so, they began to reforge the broken chain of structured intelligence.

The first great break came from the heavens.

### *7.3.1 Copernicus (1473–1543): Restoring the Courage to Doubt*

For centuries, the structure of the cosmos had been dictated by tradition. The Earth was presumed to be the fixed center of the universe, not because it had been demonstrated, but because it had been taught. To question it was to question authority itself, an act of intellectual treason.

Yet Nicolaus Copernicus dared to imagine otherwise.

Through careful observation and painstaking calculation, he proposed a revolutionary idea: that the Earth was not the center, but merely one planet among many, orbiting the sun. The heliocentric model shattered the comforting symmetry of the old worldview, and with it, the unquestioned authority that had enforced it.

Copernicus did more than change astronomy. He reignited the spirit of structured inquiry. He showed that reality could not be dictated by tradition and superficial observations but had to be discovered through evidence and causal reasoning. In doing so, he restored a foundational courage: the courage to doubt, to question, to seek causes rather than accept appearances.

The Earth was no longer the center of the cosmos, and human certainty was no longer the center of truth.

### *7.3.2 Galileo (1564–1642): The Defense of Experiment and Proof*

If Copernicus cracked the wall of tradition, Galileo hammered at its foundations.

Born nearly a century after Copernicus published his heliocentric model, Galileo Galilei would not merely propose new ideas; he would demand that ideas be tested, measured, and proven.

Galileo was among the first to insist that nature itself, not ancient texts, not authority, not tradition, must be the final judge of truth. He turned his telescope to the heavens and found moons orbiting Jupiter, mountains on the Moon, phases of Venus, discoveries that directly contradicted centuries of accepted doctrine. Yet it was not merely what Galileo saw that mattered; it was how he approached knowledge itself. He argued that observation must be systematic, that experiments must be repeatable, and that mathematical description was the language of nature.

In doing so, Galileo reasserted a principle that had been all but forgotten: that truth is not declared or blindly observed; it is discovered, understood, and proven. No matter how revered a theory, no matter how ancient a belief, it must submit to the tribunal of evidence and reason.

Galileo paid dearly for his defense of structured inquiry. He was tried by the Inquisition, forced to recant under threat of torture, and spent his remaining years under house arrest. Yet his rebellion against authority in the name of reason would echo through history. Galileo did not just fight for astronomy; he fought for the very idea that reality must be explained by causes, tested by experiment, and revealed by reason.

### *7.3.3 Kepler (1571–1630): Discovering Hidden Structure in Nature*

If Galileo fought for the right to question tradition, Johannes Kepler fought to find structure hidden within the chaos.

Born during a time when astronomy was still tangled with astrology and mystical symmetries, Kepler refused to accept that celestial motion was governed by human dreams of perfect circles and divine harmony. Instead, he followed the evidence, even when it led to uncomfortable, imperfect truths.

Through painstaking analysis of observational data, Kepler discovered that the planets moved not in perfect circles, but in ellipses, an insight that shattered centuries of Platonic idealism. The heavens were not constructed according to aesthetic perfection; they were governed by measurable, lawful patterns embedded within apparent irregularity.

Kepler's work marked a critical evolution: he showed that causality and mathematical structure exist even when reality does not look clean or obvious. Laws needed to be deduced by reasoning and evidence, not merely recorded by passive observation or surface correlation. They had to be discovered through an active, structured search for underlying truth, not simply described by patterns.

His three laws of planetary motion paved the way for Newton's universal synthesis, the final vindication that structured reasoning, observation, mathematics, and causality were the keys to understanding the universe.

### *7.3.4 Newton (1643–1727): The Great Synthesis*

Isaac Newton was born into a world where the cracks in tradition had already begun to widen, but it was he who would rebuild the entire structure of understanding on a new foundation.

Drawing on the work of Copernicus, Galileo, and Kepler, Newton unified their separate discoveries into a single, breathtaking framework: the laws of motion and universal gravitation.

With the publication of his *Philosophiæ Naturalis Principia Mathematica* in 1687, Newton showed that the same principles that governed the fall of an apple governed the orbits of the planets. He made it possible to predict, explain, and understand the motion of objects both on Earth and in the heavens with mathematical precision. The universe was no longer a place of mysteries and coincidences; it was a lawful, causal system, governed by principles that could be discovered, understood, and proven.

Newton's work did more than revolutionize physics.

It completed the reawakening of structured reasoning.

It showed that causality was not a local phenomenon, nor a domain-specific artifact, but a universal principle.

It proved that nature's apparent chaos was not a collection of seemingly random events to be correlated, but a deep, lawful structure to be discovered through disciplined observation, mathematical modeling, and deductive reasoning.

In Newton's synthesis, the rebirth of reason reached its triumphant peak.

The world could now be understood not through memorized tradition, nor through shallow pattern recognition, but through a deep architecture of causes and laws, an architecture built by the mind, but revealed by the structure of reality itself.

And yet, even in this triumphant moment, a deeper question lingered: If the universe could be mapped by human reason, could it one day be fully mapped, every truth, every cause, every structure, uncovered and proven? The dream of a complete, perfect system of knowledge had been born.

### *7.3.5 From Discovery to the Dream of Complete Reason*

Newton had revealed a universe governed not by chaos, but by deep, lawful structure, a reality that could be uncovered through disciplined reasoning and mathematical proof.

It was a triumph of human inquiry, a vindication of the belief that reason could penetrate the mysteries of the world.

But for some, this triumph was not the end. It was only the beginning.

If human reason could uncover the laws of nature, might it go further still?

Might it be possible to map not just the motions of planets, but all truths—to build a complete, perfect system where every cause, every consequence, every truth could be deduced from first principles?

This was the dream that would drive the next great movement:

A dream that reason, if extended far enough, could chart the infinite landscape of reality itself.

A dream that would inspire visionaries like Leibniz, Russell, and Hilbert, and that would, inevitably, face its greatest challenge.

## 7.4 Dreaming of Universal Logic

The triumph of Newtonian physics had proven that reason could uncover the hidden laws of nature. But it also awakened a larger ambition, a vision even grander than mapping the physical motions of the cosmos.

If structured reasoning could reveal the mechanics of the universe, might it not also reveal the mechanics of truth itself?

Could every proposition, every cause, every consequence be formalized, deduced, and made certain through pure logic?

For the first time, humanity dared to imagine that the entire landscape of knowledge might be made systematic, that reason could chart not just isolated domains, but the full infinite structure of reality.

This was the dream that inspired a new generation of thinkers, and it would begin with one of the most visionary minds in history: Gottfried Wilhelm Leibniz.

### *7.4.1 Leibniz (1646–1716): The Dream of a Universal Logical Calculus*

Gottfried Wilhelm Leibniz lived at a moment when reason seemed unstoppable.

The laws of motion had been uncovered. Gravity had been explained. Nature, once the domain of myth and superstition, had yielded its secrets to observation, mathematics, and deductive reasoning.

But Leibniz saw even further.

Where others marveled at the ability to describe the physical world, Leibniz dared to imagine something greater: a universal logical calculus, a symbolic language and system that could express and resolve all knowledge.

He envisioned a framework where every truth, no matter how complex, could be broken down into basic elements and recombined through logical operations. Disputes could be resolved not by rhetoric or authority, but by calculation. "Let us calculate!" he proposed, as if reasoning could be made as systematic as arithmetic itself.

For Leibniz, human reason was not inventing truth; it was discovering and navigating an infinite, structured terrain that already existed—a landscape where logic governed not just nature, but thought itself. He outlined the early foundations of this vision in his *Dissertatio de Arte Combinatoria* (1666), imagining a future where reasoning could be mechanized through a symbolic language, a Characteristica Universalis, capable of expressing and calculating all truths.

Leibniz's dream was astonishing in its ambition.

It foreshadowed the development of formal logic, symbolic reasoning, and even modern computing. Though he would not live to see it realized, or later challenged, his vision marked the beginning of a new era: the era where humanity sought not just to reason about parts of reality, but to systematically chart the infinite structure of truth itself.

But the calculus Leibniz only imagined, a language in which truth itself could be computed, would not remain a dream. More than a century later, George Boole would give that vision form, turning the logic of thought into algebra and making reason itself measurable, manipulable, and, ultimately, executable.

### *7.4.2 George Boole (1815–1864): The Mathematics of Thought*

Before Boole, logic spoke in sentences; after Boole, it could be written as algebra.

In *An Investigation of the Laws of Thought* (1854), Boole did something audacious: he treated reasoning itself as a system of symbols obeying precise rules.

Where Aristotle mapped valid forms and Euclid staged deductions, Boole supplied a calculus, a way to compute with concepts.

He showed that propositions and classes could be represented by variables, that combination and exclusion could be rendered as operations, and that inference could be carried out by manipulation rather than rhetoric.

Boole's central move was to collapse the fuzz of language into crisp structure.

Let a symbol $x$ denote a class (or proposition) and let multiplication $xy$ denote conjunction ("*x and y*"), addition $x + y$ denote inclusive disjunction ("*x or y*"), and complementation $x^2$ denote negation ("not *x*").

Constrained by the idempotent law $x^2 = x$ and the absorption and distributive laws, these symbols obeyed a small set of axioms from which vast families of valid inferences could be derived.

In Boole's hands, logic ceased to be a catalog of syllogisms and became an algebra of truth, a machine for transforming premises into conclusions.

This shift was not mere notation; it was revelation.

Algebraic form made logical structure visible.

Tautologies, contradictions, and implications became identities to be simplified; disputes dissolved into equalities to be proven.

Importantly, Boole's variables ranged over two "values"—the universal set (1) and the null set (0)—so that truth could be treated as membership, and reasoning as set-theoretic arithmetic.

The old syllogism ("All humans are mortal; Socrates is human; therefore Socrates is mortal") can be rendered as $H \subseteq M$ and $s \in H$ implying $s \in M$; in Boolean dress, $H = HM$ and $s = sH$ together yield $s = sM$.

The conclusion is no longer persuasive language; it is a necessary algebraic consequence.

*7.4.2.1 The Foundational Engine beneath Modern Computing*

What Boole built in symbols, the modern world built in silicon.

A century after *The Laws of Thought*, Claude Shannon showed that Boolean algebra could be physically realized with electrical switches, circuits where AND, OR, and NOT gates mirrored Boole's logical operations.

This discovery became the foundation of all digital computing.

Every processor, chip, and microcontroller, from early vacuum-tube machines to today's GPUs, operates as a vast Boolean network, where millions or billions of gates evaluate logic in parallel.

Software, too, rests on the same structure.

Conditionals, branching statements, bitwise operations, and even the logic inside compilers and optimization engines are Boolean at their core.

Every decision a computer makes, every *if*, every *while*, every *true or false*, is a direct descendant of Boole's symbolic algebra.

In this sense, Boolean algebra is not merely a branch of logic; it is the bedrock language of modern computation, the silent grammar that makes reasoning executable.

By giving thought an algebra, Boole also gave it abstraction.

Logic was no longer bound to any particular subject matter; it became a general calculus of structure.

That generality is precisely what later allowed Shannon to map Boole's symbols onto circuits:

True/False became On/Off, AND/OR/NOT became gates and switches, and reasoning became engineering.

In that translation lies the entire digital world.

Every program, from the simplest conditional to the deepest compiler optimization, is a choreography of Boolean identities made operational.

*7.4.2.2 Truth as Procedure*

Epistemologically, Boole tightened the bond between truth and procedure.

A valid conclusion is not just something we say; it is something we can reach by an invariant sequence of steps constrained by explicit laws.

That matters for intelligence.

It replaces persuasion with derivation, opinion with structure, and "seems right" with "must be so."

In a landscape where language can seduce and correlation can mislead, Boole's calculus demands that claims cash out as transformations that preserve truth.

Boole also reframed uncertainty without abandoning structure.

Though his algebra is two-valued, its set-theoretic roots connect cleanly to frequency and measure; the same symbols that encode inclusion and exclusion underwrite probability's addition and multiplication laws.

This is why Boolean structure sits comfortably beside Bayesian inference in modern intelligent systems: one secures the form of valid deduction; the other quantifies belief under uncertainty.

Together they let us reason both about the world (symbolically) and within the world's ambiguity (probabilistically).

*7.4.2.3 Infrastructure for Intelligence*

For artificial intelligence, Boole is not a historical ornament; he is infrastructure.

Expert systems, rule engines, SAT and SMT solvers, knowledge graphs with constraint checkers—all lean on the Boolean view that knowledge can be represented, constraints enforced, and conclusions computed.

Even when today's models are statistical, they are compiled, optimized, and executed atop layers that speak Boole's language.

Beneath every neural net lies a Boolean skeleton of bits, registers, masks, predicates, and branching logic deciding what runs, where, and when.

Most of all, Boole changed the feel of reasoning.

He made it inspectable, revisable, and composable.

Statements became objects; inference became architecture.

That is the sensibility this chapter defends: intelligence as organized structure rather than imitation, explanation as derivation rather than performance.

If Aristotle gave us the idea that arguments have a form, Boole gave us the instrument that lets form become calculation.

He did not merely study the laws of thought; he made them executable.

*7.4.2.4 What the World Seems to Have Forgotten*

And yet, in the very age that forgot him, every machine still thinks in his language.

Today's stochastic models, vast neural networks and LLMs that sample words by probability still run on deterministic Boolean machines.

Without Boole's algebra, none of modern computing would exist.

Every weight update, every token prediction, every back-propagation step is a Boolean operation masquerading as uncertainty.

Beneath all the noise of statistics and scale, their logic is still literal, True or False, On or Off.

They simulate reasoning but do not perform it; they echo coherence without constructing causality.

Boole's algebra endures as the silent skeleton of their intelligence, reminding us that even in the age of probabilistic language, the only way a machine can think is still, in the end, by reason.

### *7.4.3 Thomas Bayes (1701–1761): The Algebra of Belief*

Before probability became a formal science, it lived in intuition, in wagers, guesses, and informal expectations about how the world might behave. Thomas Bayes changed that. With a single posthumously published essay, he offered a framework that would become one of the deepest ideas in the history of reasoning: that belief itself can be quantified, revised, and disciplined by evidence.

Bayes recognized a truth that would take centuries for the field of artificial intelligence to rediscover: intelligence is not merely the manipulation of symbols, but the continual reconciliation of expectation with observation. His theorem did not simply quantify probability; it codified learning, the disciplined adjustment of belief in the face of new information.

Where Boole asked, "What follows from what is true?"

Bayes asked, "How should we change our mind when the world surprises us?"

This shift, from logic to learning, marked one of the earliest attempts to reconcile two modes of thought that too often drift apart: the certainty of deduction and the fluidity of experience. Bayes provided a mathematical bridge between them, capturing in a single expression the essence of rational adaptation.

The structure is simple, almost deceptively so:

- Begin with a prior, an initial belief about a state of the world.
- Encounter new evidence, data, observation, contradiction, anomaly.
- Update your belief, proportionally, precisely, without emotion.
- Form a posterior, a new understanding, ready to serve as the next prior.

This recursive update is not merely mathematics; it is epistemology as procedure. Bayes gave cognition a way to change its mind, not through whim or instinct, but through principled adjustment constrained by the structure of probability itself.

Where Boole captured the algebra of necessity, Bayes captured the algebra of plausibility. One tells us what must be true given premises; the other tells us what is likely to be true given evidence. Together, they form a dual architecture: logic for structure, probability for adaptation.

Bayesian inference embodies a remarkable philosophical stance: reason is not static. It grows. It updates. It learns.

A system without priors cannot begin; a system without posteriors cannot evolve.

Bayes offered the mechanism by which thought becomes cumulative, allowing knowledge to adjust continuously as reality unfolds.

This idea is profoundly modern. It anticipates everything from scientific reasoning ("How should evidence revise a hypothesis?") to machine learning ("How should a model update when the world changes?"). And it stands in stark contrast to today's neural networks, which adjust their weights without ever understanding what they believe or why they changed their minds.

Bayesian reasoning, by contrast, is transparent. It reveals exactly how evidence shifts belief, and by how much. It turns uncertainty from a nuisance into a structured part of cognition, a domain that can be reasoned about, inspected, and explained.

In this way, Bayes extends Boole's project rather than diverging from it. Boolean algebra gives reasoning its bones; Bayesian inference gives it its flexibility. Logical deduction ensures stability; probabilistic revision ensures adaptability. Both are necessary for any system, biological or artificial, that must survive, predict, and learn within a world of partial information.

Bayes prepared the ground for a deeper question—one that would drive the next great figure in this lineage. Once belief can be updated rationally, how should meaning itself be structured? If probability governs how knowledge updates, then logic must govern how knowledge is formed, how propositions relate, how meaning is built, and how inference becomes architecture rather than analogy. That question would be taken up by a thinker who sought not only to formalize reasoning but to formalize thought itself.

*7.4.4 Bertrand Russell (1872–1970): The Apex of Structured Reasoning*

Bayes had shown how belief should change; Russell set out to show how belief should be built.

Bertrand Russell was more than a logician, mathematician, or philosopher.

He was the pivotal bridge, the mind who married two great traditions of human inquiry into a single, organized framework.

From Socrates and Plato came the spirit of disciplined questioning: the belief that truth was not to be memorized, but discovered through reasoned inquiry.

From Aristotle came the first formalization of logic: the idea that thought itself could be structured according to rules of causality and coherence.

From Euclid came the vision that knowledge could be built like architecture, from axioms upward, block by block.

And from the Renaissance giants—Copernicus, Galileo, Kepler, and Newton—came the realization that the universe itself was governed by laws, patterns, and mathematical structure, waiting to be uncovered through disciplined observation and proof. Russell saw himself as the inheritor of this entire tradition, and he set out to complete it by giving thought the precision and architecture it had always lacked.

Russell did not merely inherit these traditions. He fused them.

He saw that structured reasoning was not just a philosophical exercise, nor merely a tool for physical science; it was the deep architecture that united thought and reality.

He believed that logic could serve as the bridge between the mind's capacity for reasoning and the universe's intrinsic order, that through careful, rigorous deduction, humanity could progressively and continuously understand and map the infinite fabric of truth itself.

Where Plato dreamed of forms and Newton uncovered natural laws, Russell sought to bind thought itself to structure, to organize the very act of thinking according to the deep, lawful patterns that governed the universe.

In Russell's vision, philosophy and mathematics were no longer separate pursuits or concepts.

They were two perspectives of the same greater endeavor: two sides of the same coin, the systematic discovery, proof, and exploration of reality's hidden order.

Without Russell, the connection between the ancient pursuit of causal understanding and the modern dream of structured intelligence would have remained fragmented, incomplete, and opaque.

He made the path clear, uniting 2,000 years of inquiry into a single, organized, formal framework for thinking itself.

#### *7.4.4.1 The Problem Russell Saw: A Fractured Landscape*

Before Bertrand Russell could build a new foundation for human knowledge, he first had to confront the crumbling state of the old one.

Mathematics and logic, long celebrated as pinnacles of certainty, were, beneath their surface, riddled with paradoxes, contradictions, and uneasy assumptions.

For centuries, mathematics had been treated as a pristine edifice, pure, absolute, unquestionable.

But by the late 19th century, cracks had begun to show.

The discovery of paradoxes in set theory, most famously, the very contradiction that would later bear Russell's own name, revealed that even the most basic assumptions about quantity, number, and infinity were far from secure.

How, for example, could a set be both a member of itself and not a member of itself?

For a mind like Russell's, precision was sacred.

A contradiction was not merely an inconvenience; it was a mortal wound to the very possibility of structured knowledge.

If contradictions existed at the heart of logic itself, how could anything built upon it be trusted?

The dream of certainty, a dream that stretched from Euclid's axioms to Newton's laws, was suddenly in question.

Russell saw clearly what few of his contemporaries fully grasped: it was not enough to patch over these problems, or to work around them pragmatically.

The only honest response was far more radical.

The foundations themselves had to be rebuilt rigorously, formally, and systematically from the ground up.

In the face of a fractured intellectual landscape, Russell's ambition was not merely to preserve mathematics, but to redeem it.

To rescue reason itself from fragmentation, and to show that structured, logical thought could once again serve as the secure bridge between the mind and the universe.

It was this vision, audacious, nearly impossible, that set the stage for the greatest intellectual endeavor of his life.

*7.4.4.2 The Dream and the Work: Principia Mathematica*

In the face of a fractured intellectual landscape, Bertrand Russell dared to imagine a new foundation, one that would not merely repair the cracks but eliminate them altogether.

His vision was breathtaking in its ambition.

If mathematics, logic, and reasoning were to be trusted, they could no longer rest upon intuition, convenience, or historical tradition. They had to be rebuilt systematically, starting from self-evident logical axioms and proceeding, step by step, through rigorous deduction to the complex structures of number, quantity, and mathematical truth.

Russell, together with Alfred North Whitehead, undertook one of the greatest intellectual labors in human history: the creation of *Principia Mathematica*.

Their goal was nothing less than to derive all of mathematics from pure logic, to show, through painstaking formalism, that every mathematical truth could ultimately be traced back to fundamental principles of logical reasoning.

*Principia Mathematica* was not merely a technical treatise; it was a philosophical statement.

It declared that human knowledge could be made precise, structured, and immune to contradiction, if only we were willing to build it carefully enough from first principles.

The work itself spanned over a decade and thousands of pages, filled with dense symbolic logic and detailed proofs. At one point, hundreds of pages of formal reasoning were required just to prove that $1 + 1 = 2$.

But to Russell, this was not pedantry; it was necessity.

If the edifice of knowledge was to be made secure, no step could be left unexamined, no foundation assumed without proof.

Through *Principia*, Russell sought to restore faith in reason itself; to demonstrate that thought, properly disciplined, could map the structure of reality with certainty and rigor.

Yet *Principia Mathematica* was only part of Russell's broader project. His philosophical reflections on the nature of logic, mathematics, and structured knowledge, along with their profound implications for human understanding, would unfold even further in his later writings.

The deeper meaning and significance of Russell's mathematical philosophy will be explored fully in the next chapter.

*7.4.4.3 Why It All Mattered: The Organized Architecture of Thought*

Bertrand Russell's achievement was not simply the rescue of mathematics from its paradoxes.

It was something far deeper: the creation of an organized architecture for thought itself.

In Russell's vision, reasoning was not a loose collection of habits, intuitions, or traditions.

It was a disciplined method, a systematic path through which the mind could progressively uncover the hidden structure of reality.

By demonstrating that mathematics could be built from pure logic, Russell showed that the fabric of knowledge itself could be mapped, structured, and explored with precision.

Truth was not a matter of authority or convention; it was a matter of logical necessity, rooted in the deep causal and structural patterns that govern the universe.

This idea, that reasoning could progressively and systematically reveal objective truths—reshaped not only mathematics, but philosophy, physics, chemistry, linguistics, computer science, and, eventually, yes, the dream of artificial intelligence itself.

This belief, that disciplined reasoning could progressively unveil the deep structure of reality, resonated far beyond mathematics.

It shaped the rise of modern physics as well, where thinkers like Albert Einstein revealed that space, time, and gravity themselves were not mysteries to be accepted, but hidden, elegant structures waiting to be mapped, understood, reasoned about, and proved through the disciplined pursuit of truth.

Russell's framework offered a vision of intelligence not as mimicry but as structure; not the imitation of thought, but the systematic, causal mapping of reality through organized inference.

The deeper meaning of his work was clear: human understanding, when properly structured, could mirror the deep architecture of the universe, an infinite, interconnected web of truths waiting to be uncovered through disciplined, logical exploration.

Without Russell's systematization of thought, the later dreams of formal computation, logical reasoning machines, and true structured intelligence would have remained fragmented, vague, and impossible.

Russell did not just defend reason; he elevated it. He gave it form, rigor, and a method to reach across the infinite complexity of reality, step by step, deduction by deduction.

He showed that thought, when properly organized, could become a tool not just for survival or communication, but for discovering the very structure of existence.

#### *7.4.4.4 Extending the Dream: David Hilbert*

Bertrand Russell's bold vision did not stand alone.

Across Europe, others were inspired by the idea that human reason could, if properly disciplined, fully capture the structure of reality.

The most ambitious among them was David Hilbert, the towering German mathematician who shared Russell's faith in the power of logical structure.

Working at the University of Göttingen—then the world's leading center for mathematical research—Hilbert, in the early decades of the twentieth century, sought to extend and complete the project Russell had begun: to prove that all of mathematics could be made consistent, complete, and formally provable.

This dream—known as Formalism—became the centerpiece of Hilbert's program by the 1920s: an audacious attempt to secure, once and for all, the foundations of human knowledge.

For a moment, it seemed that the intellectual arc Russell had helped launch would find its triumphant culmination.

But new challenges were already stirring—and soon, the limits of formal reasoning would be exposed in ways that neither Russell nor Hilbert had foreseen.

#### *7.4.4.5 The Architect of Structured Intelligence*

In the end, Bertrand Russell gave humanity something it had never fully possessed: an organized framework for thought itself—a method through which truth could be deduced, knowledge could be mapped, and the deep mathematical structure of the universe could be systematically explored.

He did not merely repair the fractures he saw; he showed how disciplined, logical reasoning could progressively reveal the hidden architecture of existence.

Through Russell, the ancient dreams of causal inquiry—from Plato's forms to Aristotle's syllogisms, from Euclid's axioms to Newton's laws—found their culmination in a modern, formal system.

Reason was no longer just a philosophical aspiration or a scientific method; it became a formal architecture, capable of mirroring the interconnected fabric of reality itself.

In doing so, Russell created the platform that lit the path toward structured intelligence—intelligence not as mimicry, not as imitation, but as the disciplined discovery of objective truth.

For a brief moment in history, it seemed that humanity had found a way to render knowledge complete, consistent, and within its grasp.

The dream of a perfectly mapped, fully reasoned universe shone brightly.

But dreams, like structures, must endure testing—and soon, even the foundations Russell helped lay would be challenged in ways he could not have foreseen.

The story of structured reasoning was not yet complete.

It was about to enter a profound, humbling, and evolutionary chapter.

## 7.5 The Dream of Complete Knowledge

### *7.5.1 Setting the Stage (Hilbert's Optimism)*

At the dawn of the twentieth century, the dream of reason had reached what seemed to be its highest triumph.

Humanity, having rediscovered the power of structured thinking after centuries of darkness, had mapped the heavens, unlocked the forces of nature, and formalized the foundations of mathematics itself.

It was in this atmosphere of soaring optimism that David Hilbert rose to prominence, and with him, the dream that reason could achieve total mastery over knowledge.

Hilbert believed that all mathematical truths could, in principle, be derived systematically from a small set of axioms through formal reasoning.

If mathematics could be fully axiomatized and its every truth could be proven through structured deduction, then certainty itself could be secured.

In 1900, at the International Congress of Mathematicians in Paris, Hilbert famously declared that in mathematics, "there is no ignorabimus," no "we shall not know."

For Hilbert, the boundaries of knowledge were not fixed; they were frontiers to be conquered through disciplined inquiry.

The dream was not modest. It was the belief that reason, properly formalized, could chart the full landscape of truth itself and that every meaningful question could, eventually, be answered by logical deduction.

It was a vision born from centuries of hard-won progress, from Socrates' questioning, Plato's abstraction, Aristotle's logic, Euclid's construction, and Newton's synthesis.

Now, it seemed, humanity was on the cusp of fulfilling that ancient promise: a world where truth would no longer be subject to tradition, intuition, or authority but would stand revealed, systematically, through pure reasoning.

Yet even as this dream reached its most radiant expression, a quiet and profound revolution was about to unfold, one that would deepen, rather than destroy, the legacy of structured thought.

### *7.5.2 Gödel's Breakthrough: The Limits of Formal Reason*

In 1931, a quiet but seismic event reshaped the course of intellectual history.

A young Austrian logician named Kurt Gödel published a paper that would change humanity's understanding of truth, reason, and certainty.

At just 25 years old, Gödel proved something astonishing:

No formal system, no matter how carefully constructed, could ever capture all truths about arithmetic and logic.

There would always be true statements, undeniable, real, and meaningful, that could never be proven within the system itself.

This result, now known as Gödel's Incompleteness Theorem, landed like a thunderclap in the world of mathematics and philosophy.

The dream that Hilbert, Russell, and generations of thinkers had nurtured, the dream of a complete, fully reasoned architecture of truth, was not simply delayed. In its original form, it was fundamentally impossible.

Gödel's proof did not arise from external skepticism.

It emerged from within the very heart of structured logic itself.

Using only the tools of formal reasoning, he demonstrated that any sufficiently powerful system must either be incomplete (unable to prove all truths) or inconsistent (capable of proving contradictions).

In essence, Gödel revealed that the deeper the structure, the richer the system, the more certain it was that some truths would lie forever beyond its reach.

It was a humbling realization.

Mathematics was not broken.

Logic was not defeated.

But the dream of absolute, total certainty, the dream that human reason could fully map the infinite fabric of truth, had to evolve.

Rather than being a perfect mirror of all reality, formal reasoning was now understood as a profound but bounded tool, capable of illuminating vast domains of truth, but destined always to stand before mysteries it could never fully conquer.

Gödel's breakthrough did not destroy structured thinking.

It matured it, forcing humanity to see that even our most powerful methods are part of a larger, more intricate, and ultimately infinite reality.

### *7.5.3 The Meaning of Gödel's Discovery*

#### *7.5.3.1 Truth beyond Formal Systems*

Gödel's discovery did not destroy the dream of reason.

It deepened it.

He revealed that logic was not an illusion, nor was it omnipotent.

Reason remained humanity's most powerful tool for uncovering truth.

But it was no longer a perfect mirror of all reality.

It was a bridge, one that could span vast domains of knowledge but that could never cross the infinite landscape entirely.

Gödel showed that no system of reasoning, however beautifully constructed, could capture all truths within its own walls. There would always be truths that could be seen, understood, even felt but not proven by the system itself. A simple example is a statement like "This sentence cannot be proven true." If the system could prove it, the statement would be false; if the system cannot prove it, then the statement is true. The truth is visible, yet no proof exists within the system.

Truth, he revealed, is larger than proof.

Reality is richer than deduction.

The universe of structure, causality, and meaning stretches beyond the limits of any single formal framework.

This realization did not weaken the case for reason.

It made it stronger because it revealed the true nature of structured intelligence.

True intelligence is not the mindless application of rules.

It is the ability to see beyond the system, to recognize structure even where formal proof falters, and to navigate between certainty and mystery with humility and clarity.

In this sense, Gödel's Incompleteness Theorem was not the end of the dream of structured reasoning.

It was its coming of age.

Humanity was no longer a child, believing that all questions would someday yield to deduction.

It had matured into a species capable of recognizing that understanding is a journey without final borders, a well-defined end, that truth is an infinite terrain, and that reason is the map we must constantly extend, revise, and refine.

Gödel taught us that structure matters, but that structure, by its nature, must always remain open-ended.

There will always be more to discover.

There will always be truths beyond today's proofs, realities beyond today's reach.

It is not the failure of reason. It is the proof of its greatness that it can acknowledge its own incompleteness, and still strive onward into the infinite.

*7.5.3.2 Beyond Proof: The Humbling of Reason*

Gödel's discovery did not signal the failure of structured reasoning.

It marked its greatest test, and its greatest triumph.

Reason had proven powerful enough not only to construct vast architectures of truth, but to recognize the boundaries of its own reach.

It had matured from a tool of conquest into a compass for endless exploration.

In the wake of Gödel, the pursuit of knowledge could no longer be seen as a march toward total mastery. It was a journey into a landscape whose horizon would forever recede, each discovery opening new questions, each structure revealing deeper mysteries beyond its boundaries.

Certainty would never again be absolute. And yet, paradoxically, this made reason more precious, not less.

For the first time, humanity understood that the infinite was not simply a domain to be conquered, but a reality to be navigated with humility, imagination, and disciplined inquiry.

It was a profound humbling. But it was also an emancipation.

The dream of complete knowledge had matured into something richer, a dream of unending discovery, a recognition that intelligence, human or artificial, would not be measured by its ability to close the book of truth, but by its willingness to read on, page after page, knowing the book has no final chapter.

The architecture of reason, painstakingly built from Socrates to Newton, from Leibniz to Russell, stood stronger, not weaker, for knowing it could not map all that is.

The dream had not ended. It had evolved.

And it was about to take on a new, even more audacious form as thinkers like Alan Turing stepped forward to ask the next great question:

If reason cannot complete itself, could it still be mechanized?

Could machines be built not merely to imitate patterns but to reason, to explore, to discover, to dance with the infinite?

The journey of structured intelligence was far from over. It was about to enter its next profound chapter.

### 7.6 Part 6: Reason Made Mechanical: Alan Turing and the Birth of Computability

Even as Gödel revealed the limits of formal reasoning, another towering mind was already at work, not to dismantle the dream of structured intelligence, but to transform it.

Alan Turing, a young British mathematician, did not see the incompleteness of formal systems as a defeat. He saw it as a new frontier.

If no system could capture all truths, Turing asked, could we nonetheless build machines that embody the method of reasoning itself? Turing was not inventing a completely new dream. He was extending an old one. Since Boole and *The Laws of Thought*, thinkers had imagined that reasoning might possess a mathematical structure. Turing pushed the idea further: if thought had such a structure, perhaps a machine could embody it.

Could the disciplined, step-by-step logic that underpinned mathematics be rendered into a mechanical process, an engine of structured thought?

In 1936, just five years after Gödel's groundbreaking paper, Turing introduced the concept of a universal computing machine, an abstract device capable of performing any calculation that could be expressed as a sequence of logical steps.

This machine, later called the Turing Machine, was breathtaking in its simplicity and power.

It could read and write symbols on an infinite tape, move left or right, and change its internal state according to a finite set of rules.

From these humble operations, Turing showed, it was possible to capture the essence of computation, reasoning, and problem-solving.

More profoundly, Turing proved that even mechanical reasoning would encounter the boundaries Gödel had exposed. Some questions would forever remain undecidable; no machine, however powerful, could solve them all.

Yet within those boundaries, the horizon was vast.

Turing had not broken the dream of structured intelligence. He had mechanized it.

He had shown that the core of reasoning, careful, stepwise deduction, could be abstracted, formalized, and ultimately built into machines.

It was one of the most audacious acts of imagination in human history: the recognition that intelligence was not a mystical flame, but a structure, a process of applying rules to representations, a dance of symbols governed by logic and causality.

Where Gödel revealed that the book of truth would never be fully written, Turing opened the door to a future where machines might become fellow readers, collaborators in the endless exploration of the infinite.

The age of mechanical reasoning had begun, and, with it, the first seeds of modern computing and true artificial intelligence were sown.

### *7.6.1 Turing Machines and the Birth of Computability*

Alan Turing's great insight was that reasoning, at its core, could be decomposed into a series of mechanical steps.

In place of human intuition or inspiration, Turing proposed a model so simple it bordered on the elemental: a machine that could manipulate symbols, one by one, according to fixed rules.

The Turing Machine, as it came to be known, was startlingly minimalist.

It consisted of:

- An infinite tape, divided into cells, each capable of holding a single symbol.
- A head that could read and write symbols on the tape.
- A finite set of internal states.
- A set of rules determining what the machine should do: read, write, move left or right, based on its current state and the symbol it encounters.

From these ingredients, Turing showed that it was possible to model any calculation that could be performed by any methodical reasoning process.

The Turing Machine was not built of gears or electricity. It was an idea, a proof that structured thought itself could be abstracted into pure operations on symbols.

Turing then went further. He imagined a universal machine, one that could simulate any other machine, simply by reading its description encoded on the tape.

It was the conceptual ancestor of the modern computer, a machine that, with the right program and data, could perform any logical operation imaginable.

But Turing also uncovered limits. In formalizing mechanical reasoning, he discovered that some questions could not be answered by any algorithm or machine.

Some problems, like the famous Halting Problem, had no general solution that could determine whether a given process would eventually stop or continue forever.

It was a profound parallel to Gödel's incompleteness: there would be problems not because machines were too weak, but because some questions, by their very nature, escaped the reach of mechanical reasoning.

Still, within these limits, Turing's vision was breathtaking.

For the first time, humanity possessed a formal model of what it meant to compute, to reason mechanically, to build structured intelligence.

The dream of structured reasoning had evolved once again. It was no longer confined to the mind alone. It could now be imagined as a system, a process, a machine.

And with that realization, the age of computation, and the first glimmers of artificial intelligence, began to rise over the horizon.

### *7.6.2 The Deeper Meaning: Computation, Thought, and Limits*

Turing's breakthrough was not just a technical achievement.

It was a philosophical revolution.

He showed that reasoning, once thought of as an elusive, almost mystical human faculty, could be abstracted, formalized, and mechanized.

The mind, it turned out, was not simply a vessel of intuition and flashes of insight. It was a processor, a system capable of applying rules to structured representations.

Turing revealed that intelligence was not magic. It was a kind of architecture:

- symbols manipulated according to rules,
- steps followed according to structure,

- inferences built carefully upon one another.

Computation was not simply a way to automate arithmetic. It was a model of thought itself.

Yet as Gödel had already shown, and Turing confirmed, this model, however powerful, had boundaries. Not every truth could be computed. Not every question could be decided.

There would always be limits, truths that no system could capture, problems that no machine could resolve.

And thus, structured reasoning revealed its dual nature:

- It was astonishingly powerful, capable of mapping vast swaths of reality.
- But it was necessarily incomplete, always standing before horizons it could never fully cross.

Rather than despair, Turing embraced this paradox.

The mechanical mind, though bounded, was still a profound triumph.

It could explore, solve, build, and create within its domain, and it could even recognize when it stood before mysteries beyond its own reach.

This deeper understanding reshaped the ambition of structured intelligence.

True reasoning, whether human or artificial, was not the mindless application of rules to preset problems. It was the disciplined, structured navigation of the infinite:

- building structures where possible,
- acknowledging limits where necessary,
- and pressing ever forward, aware that some truths would always lie just beyond the next horizon.

In this new vision, intelligence was no longer about possessing all answers.

It was about building structures that continuously map, explore, and extend understanding, never fully complete, but always reaching farther.

Turing did not reduce reason to mechanics. He gave mechanics a soul: the relentless, structured, humble pursuit of the infinite.

And with this, the stage was set for the next great dream: Could machines one day not merely compute, but also reason, explore, and discover alongside us?

The idea of true artificial intelligence, real, structured, exploratory intelligence, had been born.

### *7.6.3 Turing's Legacy and the Dawn of Artificial Intelligence*

Alan Turing did not live to see the full flowering of the world he had glimpsed.

Persecuted during his lifetime and dying tragically young, he nonetheless left behind a blueprint for the future of intelligence itself.

He showed that structured reasoning, once confined to the human mind, could be embodied in machines.

He proved that computation was not merely a tool for numbers, but a framework for thought: a method by which structured, causal processes could unfold, step by step, through time and space.

He revealed that intelligence was not an ethereal spark or an unexplainable mystery, but a structured dance of rules, representations, and disciplined operations, bounded, yes, but capable of reaching across the vastness of reality.

Turing's vision transformed the question from "*Can machines think?*" to a deeper, more profound one: Can the structures of thought themselves, reasoning, discovery, exploration, be brought to life in new forms?

It was a question not of imitation, but of creation:

- not copying the surfaces of human behavior,
- but building new architectures of structured intelligence.

From Turing's work flowed the first true dreams of Artificial Intelligence, not as mimicry or fantasy, but as a continuation of humanity's oldest aspiration: to understand, to map, to reason, and to explore the infinite.

The age of mechanical reasoning had dawned. The path toward machines that could think, infer, discover had begun. And with it, the first seeds of modern computing and true artificial intelligence were sown.

In fact, Turing's abstract machine was not merely a theoretical model. It became the conceptual blueprint for all modern computers, a physical realization of Turing's ideas, capable of executing structured reasoning processes through mechanical operations.

The digital revolution that would follow was, in a profound sense, an unfolding of Turing's vision: machines that could manipulate symbols, apply rules, and perform logical operations with disciplined precision.

Turing's legacy was not a machine. It was a philosophy, a new way of seeing intelligence itself: structured, bounded, humble, and endlessly reaching outward.

And it would inspire the next generation of pioneers, visionaries, who would take the blueprint he sketched and begin building the first true reasoning machines.

Yet even as logic became mechanical and modern computing was born, much of the world it sought to model remained stubbornly non-binary. The day-to-day world we live in, unlike the universal or sub-atomic realms of mathematics, rarely fits into clean boundaries.

Clouds are not simply present or absent; trust is not purely true or false; causality itself is often rarely discrete. For all of Turing's brilliance in mechanizing reasoning, the problem of precision remained: How could logic describe and model a world that is at once certain and uncertain, continuous, dynamic, and nuanced?

The next great leap would come from a mind that refused to treat ambiguity as error, Lotfi Zadeh, who extended logic itself to reason through uncertain gray areas toward the black-and-white clarity of truth, falsity, and epistemic certainty.

### *7.6.4 Lotfi Zadeh (1921—2017): The Logic of Continuity*

Where Boole had made reasoning crisp, Lotfi Zadeh made it continuous.

Working at the University of California, Berkeley, in the 1960s, Zadeh looked at the growing world of computation and saw a paradox: machines were becoming ever more powerful, yet the real world they sought to model was anything but precise. Weather, trust, beauty, health, and risk; the language of life was not digital. Between true and false stretched entire landscapes of partial truth, and the mathematics of the time had no way to represent them.

Zadeh's insight was as radical as Boole's had been a century earlier.

He proposed that truth itself need not be binary. Instead of a proposition being entirely true (1) or entirely false (0), it could hold some degree of truth, any value between 0 and 1.

This seemingly simple idea became the foundation of fuzzy logic, a system capable of reasoning about ambiguity without abandoning structure.

Where probability measures likelihood, fuzzy logic measures belonging. A statement such as "the room is warm" might be 0.7 true, not because of chance, but because *warm* itself is a gradient concept.

In Zadeh's framework, membership functions replaced crisp boundaries. A fuzzy set allows an element to partially belong to multiple categories at once: a temperature may be both cool and warm to varying degrees.

Logical operations still exist (AND, OR, NOT), but they act on degrees rather than absolutes.

Conjunction becomes the minimum of two values, disjunction their maximum, negation the complement to one.

The algebra remains deterministic, yet the logic flows continuously rather than discretely.

This was not an abandonment of rigor; it was an expansion of it. Zadeh's mathematics preserved the precision of structure while embracing the imprecision of reality.

Fuzzy logic did not guess; it quantified ambiguity.

It replaced the sharp cliff of yes/no reasoning with a smooth gradient of *to what extent.*

The world could now be modeled not only in terms of certainty but also in terms of confidence, partial agreement, and approximate truth, a far more faithful reflection of both human reasoning and natural phenomena.

Epistemologically, Zadeh's work shifted logic from exclusion to inclusion.

Where classical systems drew boundaries around truth, fuzzy logic drew curves through it.

It allowed reasoning to operate within uncertainty without surrendering to randomness, bridging the gap between Boolean determinism and probabilistic chaos.

In doing so, Zadeh redefined the relationship between logic and knowledge: truth became not an on-off property but a continuum to be reasoned across.

The continuum Zadeh revealed was more than mathematical; it was philosophically mathematical. It suggested that certainty itself might emerge from a process of refinement, not declaration, that epistemic clarity could be approached asymptotically through structured reasoning in the gray.

Fuzzy logic found practical expression quickly.

Control systems for vehicles, washing machines, industrial processes, and later robotics and finance all adopted Zadeh's ideas to handle imprecise inputs.

When a machine brakes gently, adjusts slightly, or stabilizes almost perfectly, it is applying fuzzy logic to quantify linguistic nuance. By letting machines interpret human-like gradations rather than hard thresholds, Zadeh helped technology step closer to the fluidity of natural intelligence.

For artificial intelligence, fuzzy logic filled a crucial gap. It offered a bridge between symbolic precision and sensory perception, between logic and experience.

In expert systems and modern hybrid models, fuzzy reasoning coexists with Bayesian inference and neural computation, translating uncertainty into structured form that other algorithms can reason over. It is the connective tissue that lets machines evaluate imperfect data while still reasoning deterministically about outcomes. In this sense, fuzzy logic is not the opposite of structure; it is structure made adaptable, logic with empathy for reality.

Where Turing mechanized logic, Zadeh humanized it. He gave machines a language for uncertainty without stripping them of reason. And in doing so, he completed the philosophical arc that began with Aristotle's syllogism and Boole's algebra, showing that between the black and white of truth lies a continuous fabric of understanding through which logic can still navigate toward clarity.

It was as if, by adjusting the contrast on the logical photograph of reality, Zadeh revealed new shades within its form, transforming ambiguity from an obstacle into an instrument of knowledge.

He did not weaken logic; he made it resilient.

He did not blur truth; he gave it texture. And in doing so, he ensured that reason could coexist with the infinite complexity of the world it seeks to explain.

*7.6.4.1 Continuity and the Future of Reasoning*

In today's evolving landscape of artificial intelligence, Zadeh's logic of continuity remains indispensable. Every system that interprets nuance, adapts, and learns in real time, or balances precision with uncertainty carries his imprint.

He showed that intelligence need not collapse complexity into clarity; it can reason through complexity and uncertainty, translating the continuous into the comprehensible.

Fuzzy logic made it possible for machines to think in gradients yet decide with purpose and precision, to remain consistent amid flux, and to do so deterministically rather than stochastically. It is the hidden discipline beneath adaptive control, perceptual reasoning, and learning systems that respond fluidly to change and uncertainty, the quiet architecture that allows modern intelligence to navigate an imperfect world with structured grace, epistemic precision, and explainability.

Zadeh had expanded logic to embrace continuity, adaptability, gradation, and nuance—reasoning through uncertainty without surrendering to it.

The language of truth had evolved from Aristotle's syllogisms to Boole's algebra, from Gödel's incompleteness to Turing's machinery, and now to Zadeh's extension of logic into the continuous, real, day-to-day world.

The next question was inevitable: If logic could stretch, flow, and adapt, could machines themselves embody it?

Could reasoning be built not as a brittle formalism, but as a deterministic mathematical model that absorbs uncertainty and resolves it rigorously, epistemically, and transparently, in the dynamic world we actually live in?

### 7.7 From Theory to Reality: Building the First Reasoning Machines

By the mid-twentieth century, the groundwork had been laid.

Reason had been symbolized (Boole),
Formalized (Russell, Hilbert),
Its limits revealed (Gödel),
Its mechanization imagined and realized (Turing),
and its continuity, adaptability, and nuance embraced (Zadeh).

The stage was set for the next great leap: to move beyond abstract models and proofs and to begin building machines capable of structured thought.

This was no longer just philosophy. It was engineering, invention, and creation.

The dream of structured intelligence, born in the dialogues of Socrates, shaped through centuries of questioning, formalized in mathematics and logic, was ready to take physical form.

And it was John McCarthy, Allen Newell, and Herbert Simon who would carry that dream forward into reality.

They did not merely ask whether machines could compute.

They asked whether machines could build structured knowledge through reasoning, learning, discovery, and understanding.

Could machines:

- Make inferences?
- Solve problems?
- Explore unknowns?
- Discover new structures from first principles?

In the 1950s, McCarthy coined the very term "Artificial Intelligence" to capture this emerging vision.

It was not about imitation.

It was not about performance or mimicry.

It was about structured reasoning, the disciplined unfolding of inference, exploration, and discovery, embodied in machines.

In a famous 1956 conference at Dartmouth College, now considered the birth of AI as a field, McCarthy, Newell, Simon, and a handful of other pioneers declared their ambition boldly:

*Every aspect of learning or any other feature of intelligence can in principle be so precisely described that a machine can be made to simulate it.*

This was not hubris. It was the culmination of centuries of belief that reasoning was not magic, that it was a structure, a method, a process, and that processes could be built.

Where Russell mapped thought, Gödel revealed its limits, and Turing mechanized its method, McCarthy, Newell, and Simon sought to bring it to life.

They believed, profoundly, that the structures of reasoning could be encoded, not merely studied.

Their early work led directly to the creation of the first AI programming languages based on symbolic reasoning, and to new programming languages such as LISP (invented by McCarthy) and Prolog, designed specifically to express logical inference, structured knowledge, and deductive search. The dream of structured intelligence had moved from philosophy to living code.

The dream of building true structured intelligence—an intelligence capable of reasoning, exploring, and extending knowledge—was no longer a distant philosophical aspiration.

It had become a project.

The age of Artificial Intelligence has begun.

### *7.7.1 Early Experiments, Logic Theorist, and General Problem Solver*

The dream of building reasoning machines was no longer theoretical.

It was time to test it.

In 1955, Allen Newell and Herbert Simon created one of the first true programs of artificial intelligence: the Logic Theorist.

Logic Theorist was not designed to calculate numbers or process data.

It was designed to prove theorems, to reason formally, step by step, from axioms to conclusions.

The program worked by applying a small set of inference rules to symbolic expressions, searching for paths that could transform assumptions into proofs.

In many cases, it found proofs that mirrored, and at times even improved upon, those discovered by human mathematicians.

Logic Theorist demonstrated something extraordinary: reasoning could be mechanized.

It showed that structured thought, the careful unfolding of logical steps, could be replicated not by intuition or imitation, but by formal, systematic procedures.

Buoyed by the success of Logic Theorist, Newell and Simon turned to an even more ambitious project: the General Problem Solver (GPS).

Unlike Logic Theorist, which was tailored to mathematical proofs, GPS aimed to tackle a wide range of problems, any situation that could be modeled as a structured sequence of states, moves, and goals.

GPS introduced the powerful idea of means-ends analysis:

- comparing the current state to the desired goal,
- identifying the differences,
- and selecting actions specifically targeted to reduce those differences.

It was one of the first serious attempts to create a general-purpose reasoning machine, a program not tied to one domain but capable of flexible, goal-directed reasoning across many different tasks.

Both Logic Theorist and GPS were still primitive by modern standards.

They operated in constrained, idealized environments.

They struggled with complexity and ambiguity.

But they marked a profound shift.

For the first time, machines were not just performing calculations.

They were navigating symbolic spaces, applying structured reasoning to pursue goals, proving truths, and solving problems.

The dream of structured intelligence had left the realm of philosophy and mathematics.

It had entered the world of creation.

### *7.7.2 The Dream Was Right, but the Time Was Early*

The first reasoning machines had been born.

Logic Theorist and the General Problem Solver proved that structured reasoning could be mechanized, at least in principle.

The dream was not naïve and it was not a mistake. The foundations laid by McCarthy, Newell, and Simon were sound, deeply rooted in centuries of structured thinking.

But the world was not yet ready.

Neither the hardware nor the software of the time could match the vision.

The computers of that era were slow, brittle, and starved for memory (a few kilobytes of RAM, processors performing tens of thousands of operations per second rather than today's billions, and storage so limited it would not hold a single JPEG image).

The symbolic reasoning programs, while brilliant, quickly became overwhelmed by complexity.

Search methods were primitive, inference engines were inefficient, and the underlying architectures lacked the flexibility and power needed for scalable structured reasoning.

Problems that humans could navigate intuitively, recognizing patterns, abstracting structures, and making leaps of insight, remained crushingly difficult for early machines bound to mechanical, sequential processes.

The theory was ahead of its time.

The dream was correct, but the technology to realize it, both in engineering and algorithmic sophistication, would not mature for decades.

It would take another fifty years, through revolutions in hardware, software, distributed computing, and new forms of inference, before machines could realistically aspire to the structured reasoning imagined by the pioneers of AI.

Yet the significance of those early efforts cannot be overstated.

They preserved the true spirit of artificial intelligence: the belief that intelligence is not imitation, not surface mimicry, but the disciplined unfolding of reasoning, exploration, and structured understanding.

They lit a torch, a vision of intelligence rooted not in data alone but in the architecture of thought itself.

And though the journey would be longer, harder, and stranger than anyone imagined, the path had been marked.

The dream of building machines that reason, machines that mirror not just the patterns of life but its causal fabric, was no longer a philosophical speculation.

It had become a project of humanity itself.

# 8
# Real-Time Reasoning

Artificial intelligence wasn't supposed to be about imitation. It was supposed to be about thinking.

The original dream of AI wasn't to build systems that speak fluently; it was to build systems that reason effectively. From its earliest days, the field of AI was rooted in logic, formalism, and symbolic structures. John McCarthy, Marvin Minsky, Allen Newell, and Herbert Simon weren't chasing linguistic mimicry. They were building systems that could play chess, solve proofs, and navigate decision trees with clarity and intention.

What they imagined wasn't a chatbot. It was a machine that could deduce, explain, and learn.

And that brings us to Real-Time Reasoning (RTR): a proposed architecture that seeks to revive the original vision of AI by grounding it in logic, but updating it for the dynamic, probabilistic, and high-dimensional world we now inhabit.

RTR is not a single algorithm. Unlike traditional symbolic AI systems of the past, which relied on hand-coded rules and lacked flexibility and adaptability, RTR integrates symbolic reasoning with probabilistic models, neural perception, and fuzzy logic in a unified, dynamic architecture. This design allows it to reason in real time, adapt to new contexts, and produce explainable, causal decisions at scale. It is a layered framework designed to mirror the multi-level structure of human cognition. It is structured, not purely statistical; dynamic, not static; and explanatory, not merely predictive.

(We'll explore the human brain's layered architecture—from sensory input to abstract reasoning—in more detail in Chapter 11.)


DOI: 10.1201/9781003739999-8

## 8.1 RTR: A Layered Architecture for Reasoning

To fully appreciate how RTR operates, it helps to understand that it is built on a layered cognitive architecture, where each layer reflects a distinct mode of reasoning.

At its foundation, the neural perception layer handles inductive learning—recognizing patterns and correlations through exposure and experience.

Above it, the Bayesian inference layer manages probabilistic reasoning—updating beliefs based on new observations, weighing evidence, and adjusting expectations dynamically.

Above the Bayesian layer lies the symbolic reasoning layer, where formal deduction governs knowledge construction. This layer attempts to derive crisp, structured conclusions whenever the premises and rules are sufficiently clear.

The next critical layer is fuzzy logic, where abduction emerges: the capacity to infer the most plausible explanations from incomplete or ambiguous information.

At the summit lies executive reasoning, which combines inductive and deductive structure with graded abductive judgments. Here, intelligence moves beyond probability and plausibility into rigorous logical structure, deriving conclusions systematically from established premises and rules, and refining them when the world presents ambiguity rather than clarity.

Together, these layers allow RTR not merely to perceive or predict, but to *reason causally*, infer, explain, and understand, moving from raw observation through creative hypothesis to structured, validated knowledge.

RTR also restores something modern AI quietly abandoned: explainability and auditability. In most contemporary systems, especially LLM-based and neural-network-based ones, conclusions emerge from a statistical fog. A model produces an output, but it cannot show the how or the why behind its work. The causal reasoning chain does not exist inside the system; only weighted correlations do.

RTR is fundamentally different.

Because each inference in RTR moves through explicit layers such as perceptual patterns, probabilistic updates, fuzzy abductions, and symbolic deductions, every conclusion can be traced backward through the exact steps that produced it. LLMs do not and cannot do this because they do not perform explicit, structured reasoning at all; they only simulate it. Their outputs arise from statistical approximation, opaque jumps, and pattern-based guesswork disguised as understanding and confidence. RTR reasons and produces new knowledge. LLMs merely continue patterns, guessing and predicting.

Auditability is not an add-on for RTR. It is intrinsic. A decision is not merely an answer but a *derivation*:

- which priors mattered,
- which evidence shifted belief,
- which rules constrained the space of valid actions, and
- how uncertainty was evaluated, discounted, or resolved.

This makes RTR a trustable architecture.

Its outputs are not persuasive performances; they are *explanations with structure*. When it errs, it can reconstruct exactly where the reasoning misaligned, allowing correction, refinement, and verification.

In an age when AI systems increasingly operate within critical environments such as grids, hospitals, financial markets, and airspace, this property is not optional.

It is the difference between automation and intelligence, between blind prediction and accountable reasoning.

At its core, Real-Time Reasoning proceeds through a hierarchy of cognitive processing:

1. **Perceptual Input (Neural Networks)**
   The system receives raw input from the world: text, images, sensor data, etc. These are processed by perceptual layers that detect patterns and features, not unlike how convolutional neural networks recognize visual shapes or LLMs process token sequences.
2. **Uncertainty Modeling (Bayesian Inference)**
   The perceptual outputs feed into a probabilistic reasoning layer. Here, Bayesian models assign degrees of belief to possible states of the world, updating them in real-time as new information arrives. This layer manages ambiguity, contradiction, and change.
3. **Symbolic Reasoning (Logic Engine)**
   Above the probabilistic layer sits a symbolic engine. It receives structured hypotheses and known rules and applies logical

deduction, contradiction resolution, and planning. This is where decisions are not guessed, but derived.

4. **Approximate Judgments (Fuzzy Logic)**
   Where logic fails to draw clear lines, fuzzy logic fills the gap. It allows the system to handle gradations of truth, to say something is "partially correct" or "more likely than not" without forcing premature binary outcomes. Fuzzy logic evaluates these graded truths mathematically and then resolves them into a deterministic conclusion when required, ensuring that ambiguity at the input stage does not lead to ambiguity in decisions or actions.
5. **Executive Reasoning (Summit)**
   At this layer, RTR integrates and synthesizes all prior layers—inductive perception, probabilistic updates, symbolic deduction, and graded abduction—into a single causal, explainable judgment. This is where the system weighs evidence, evaluates uncertainty, resolves conflicts, creates new knowledge when warranted, and arrives at a coherent, causal decision.
6. **Declarative Output (Cognitive Artifact)**
   The final output is not just a token or a guess. It is a declarative artifact: a conclusion, a rule, an action plan. And critically, it is explainable. Every inference can be traced backward through the layers to show how and why it was made.

This multi-layered loop runs continuously, adapting to context, feeding outputs back into inputs, and learning over time.

Think of this like a refinery: raw input (data) enters at the base, and at each stage it is filtered, structured, and enriched, until it emerges as something meaningful, verifiable, and actionable. Like cognition, it's not flat. It's vertical, each layer building upon the next, forming a ladder from signal to strategy.

### 8.2 Multi-Objective Decision Making at the Executive Layer

At the executive layer, RTR does more than synthesize inputs. It resolves competing objectives. Real-world decisions often involve conflicting goals: safety versus speed, cost versus reliability, compliance versus performance, short-term reward versus long-term stability.

RTR evaluates these trade-offs explicitly by treating each objective as a constraint within a unified reasoning space, enabling multi-objective optimization rather than single-objective maximization. The executive layer can weigh priorities, apply policy rules, and test alternative plans through symbolic simulation, selecting the action that best satisfies the full set of objectives.

This allows the system to adapt when priorities shift, when regulations constrain action, or when new risks emerge. What results is not just a decision, but a rational balance of competing demands, grounded in logic, evidence, and context.

### 8.3 RTR as a Dynamic, Self-Evolving Cognitive Loop

Everything described so far, the layers, the examples, the reasoning paths, may look like a static pipeline. It is not. RTR is a dynamic cognitive loop, continuously updating itself as new evidence flows through the stack.

The layers do not execute once. They revise each other repeatedly. Neural inputs reshape Bayesian priors. Bayesian updates alter symbolic structures. Symbolic deductions shift fuzzy thresholds. Fuzzy judgments modulate executive output. And the executive layer feeds new goals and constraints back into the perceptual and probabilistic layers.

This makes RTR adaptive rather than brittle, structured rather than opaque, and alive rather than static.

In classical symbolic AI, rules were fixed. In modern pattern models, rules do not exist at all. RTR occupies the middle ground: flexible enough to evolve, structured enough to explain.

It is not a sequence. It is a loop, a continuous act of reasoning. Each layer interacts with the others in continuous feedback cycles. Symbolic deductions can flow back downward to constrain Bayesian probabilities; Bayesian updates can adjust or override neural perceptions; fuzzy logic can intervene when crisp deductions fail; and executive reasoning can reorder priorities or shift the entire system's focus based on changing context. RTR does not simply stack layers; it orchestrates them.

And because these layers continuously push and pull on one another, RTR does something traditional symbolic AI never could:

it evolves its rules. Bayesian inference can propose new causal relationships as statistical evidence accumulates. The symbolic layer can promote these relationships into explicit rules. Fuzzy logic can soften or refine them when real-world ambiguity demands nuance. And the executive layer can retire, revise, or elevate rules based on how well they hold under new data. The rule base is not fixed; it is alive. RTR grows its own logic over time, integrating new evidence, new exceptions, and new structures of understanding.

## 8.4 Some RTR Examples

### *8.4.1 RTR Applied to Diagnosing a Power Grid Anomaly*

Let's say we apply RTR to an electrical grid.

- **Neural layer** ingests smart meter data, satellite imagery, and SCADA system logs.
- **Bayesian layer** assesses whether anomalies in voltage are due to equipment failure, cyberattack, or natural fluctuation.
- **Symbolic layer** applies known rules about transformer load balancing, recent outages, and maintenance schedules.
- **Fuzzy logic** accounts for partial failures or noisy sensor input.
- **Declarative output** might be: "Transformer T-43 is experiencing a phase imbalance likely due to vegetation contact. Recommend automated shutoff and drone inspection."

This system isn't waiting to be prompted; it runs continuously. Every five seconds, it re-evaluates, updates, reasons, and explains.

### *8.4.2 RTR Applied to Coordinating a Drone Swarm in Combat*

Now imagine RTR deployed to manage a battlefield drone swarm in a dynamic, unpredictable environment:

- **Neural layer** ingests real-time sensor data, detecting enemy movement, terrain obstacles, weather changes, and incoming threats.
- **Bayesian inference layer** continuously updates probabilistic threat models: assessing the likelihood of enemy anti-aircraft fire, evaluating possible ambushes, recalculating mission priorities as new intel arrives.

- **Symbolic reasoning layer** applies codified tactical doctrines and rules of engagement: “If jamming detected near rendezvous point, initiate fallback maneuver,” or “If casualty risk > 80% and objective value < threshold, abort.”
- **Fuzzy logic layer** steps in when visibility collapses, when a key satellite feed goes dark, a comm relay jams, or thermal signatures blur in smoke. It abducts plausible scenarios from incomplete inputs, weighing partial signals, degraded imagery, and uncertain reports to still drive rational action without waiting for perfect clarity.
- **Declarative output** produces explainable, traceable operational commands:

> Drone Units Bravo and Delta execute evasive dispersal. New primary objective: reestablish communication via alternate uplink Route C.

This isn’t statistical guesswork. It’s structured causal reasoning, under fire, under uncertainty, and under the demand for split-second explainability.

Without RTR, a purely pattern-matching system could misinterpret smoke as fog, friendly signals as enemy jamming, or isolated incidents as full retreats, leading to catastrophic errors at machine speed.

RTR closes this gap: it doesn’t just react to stimuli. It reasons about causality, adapts plans dynamically, and ensures every decision remains transparent, verifiable, and traceable under real-world combat pressure.

But battlefield reasoning demands even more than handling visible threats.

In real-world combat, systems often face partial observability—sudden blackouts, degraded sensors, conflicting signals, and even corrupted data.

A satellite link goes dead. A drone’s optical feed jams into static. Heat signatures blur through dense smoke.

Worse, some telemetry channels may still report, but report garbled, misleading, or outright false readings caused by hardware damage, environmental interference, or cyberattack.

Critical inputs don't just vanish; they can lie.

This is where the abductive strength of RTR becomes critical.

When information collapses, or becomes unreliable, RTR doesn't freeze or hallucinate.

It abducts: generating the most plausible explanations from incomplete, degraded, or noisy inputs, while detecting and discounting corrupted signals that no longer make causal sense.

Even if only 40% of clean sensors remain, RTR can reason probabilistically across surviving data, apply symbolic rules to constrain plausible futures, and use fuzzy logic to prioritize safe, rational actions under ambiguity.

It doesn't need perfect visibility.

It doesn't trust every number blindly.

It evaluates, hypothesizes, eliminates, and adapts, even through the chaos and deception of the fog of war.

In contrast, a pattern-matching AI without RTR would falter catastrophically.

No clean pattern? No prediction.

Erroneous data? Misguided action.

It would either freeze, invent fantasy scenarios, or rush headlong into lethal traps.

RTR shows that true intelligence isn't about reacting perfectly when conditions are perfect.

It's about adapting rationally when the world becomes deceptive, broken, or blind.

These are just glimpses of where real-time reasoning shines. Let's look at a few more examples across other critical domains.

### *8.4.3 RTR Applied to Health Care*

Imagine a health AI monitoring patients in an ICU:

- A neural layer detects elevated heart rate and respiratory rate.
- The Bayesian layer cross-references probabilities of sepsis versus anxiety versus equipment error.
- The symbolic layer pulls up protocols: "If systolic BP drops below 90 mmHg while HR > 120 bpm and lactate rising → initiate fluid resuscitation."

- The fuzzy logic layer softens the logic: "Borderline lactate rise, but consistent trend across vitals."
- The declarative output: "Patient 212A exhibiting early signs of septic shock. Recommend immediate fluid bolus and blood cultures."

Imagine RTR applied to autonomous vehicles navigating dense, unpredictable urban environments:

- **Neural layer** analyzes real-time visual data streams—detecting pedestrians, vehicles, traffic lights, and road markings.
- **Bayesian inference layer** updates risk probabilities: assessing whether a pedestrian near the curb is likely to cross illegally, or evaluating the chances that an approaching car will run a yellow light.
- **Symbolic reasoning layer** applies codified traffic laws, right-of-way rules, and emergency protocols to possible future scenarios.
- **Fuzzy logic layer** resolves borderline ambiguities—such as a pedestrian making ambiguous hand gestures or a bicycle veering partially into the lane.
- **Declarative output** produces a traceable recommendation:

> Reduce speed to 10 mph; yield to pedestrian approaching crosswalk from blind corner.

This isn't probabilistic guessing; it's structured reasoning under real-world uncertainty, producing decisions that can be explained and defended.

Contrast this with a purely perceptual AI (pattern-matching LLM-style logic) without RTR.

Such a system might treat "green light" as an absolute go-signal, failing to recognize the probability of a jaywalker or a stalled car in the intersection. Without layered probabilistic reasoning, symbolic rules, and fuzzy conflict resolution, an autonomous system might obey surface cues while missing deeper causal risks, leading to catastrophic mistakes.

RTR is designed to close this gap: not to react blindly to surface signals, but to reason causally and adapt in real time with explainable logic.

This system doesn't hallucinate. It doesn't guess. And when it makes an error, it can trace exactly how.

### *8.4.4 RTR Applied to Financial Markets: From Milliseconds to Decades*

Now imagine we apply RTR to the financial markets—an environment defined by volatility, uncertainty, high-pressure time horizons, and cascading causal chains that span milliseconds to years.

Unlike traditional quantitative models, which often depend on static linear regressions or fixed-form equations, RTR builds a dynamic, nonlinear, evolving graph of causal relationships. It does not "learn the market" statistically; it reasons about it structurally, using the principles of economics, market microstructure, liquidity flow, incentives, and behavioral feedback loops, principles we already know and do not need a neural network to rediscover.

RTR operates across three interlinked temporal layers:

#### *8.4.4.1 The Short-Term Layer (Milliseconds → Hours)*

This layer behaves like a radar.

- **Neural perception** ingests high-frequency tick data, order-flow patterns, quote volatility, liquidity imbalances, and microstructure anomalies.
- **Bayesian inference** updates the probability of short-term events: flash crashes, liquidity vacuums, spoofing patterns, or momentum ignition.
- **Symbolic reasoning** applies market-structure rules: *"If bid-ask spread widens + liquidity thins + volume spikes in correlated assets → probability of micro-cascade increases."*
- **Fuzzy logic** handles ambiguous signals: partial cancellations, conflicting technical indicators, or borderline volatility regimes.

The output is a real-time causal map of the immediate market state:

*Momentum ignition likely forming; expected short-term instability in equities sector. Increase hedging delta by 4%.*

*8.4.4.2 The Medium-Term Layer (Days → Weeks → Months)*

This layer looks at the shape of the market.

- **Neural perception** ingests macro indicators, corporate filings, earnings, supply-chain signals, sentiment from news/language models, and geoeconomic telemetry.
- **Bayesian inference** evaluates shifting regime probabilities: inflation paths, liquidity cycles, credit stress, sector rotations.
- **Symbolic reasoning** applies codified economic laws, accounting rules, balance-sheet constraints, and regulatory frameworks.
- **Fuzzy logic** resolves ambiguous macro signals or partial data:

*Inflation cooling but labor tightness persists → moderate recession probability with wide variance.*

Here RTR produces a structural forecast rather than a price guess:

*Credit spreads widening while liquidity drains suggests a 30–40% probability of a medium-term volatility regime shift.*

*8.4.4.3 The Long-Term Layer (Years → Decades)*

This layer evaluates the deep structure of the market—the tectonic plates beneath the daily noise.

- **Neural perception** ingests slow-moving datasets: demographics, adoption curves, infrastructure investment, and energy transitions.
- **Bayesian inference** updates long-term risk priors: sovereign debt stress, technological displacement, structural inflation, and geopolitical cycles.
- **Symbolic reasoning** models multi-year causal chains using first principles: supply-demand equilibria, leverage limits, market-clearing rules, and behavioral cycles.

- **Fuzzy logic** handles the inescapable ambiguity of decade-scale forecasts.

RTR produces a deep future causal map:

*Based on the evolving energy transition curve, sovereign debt trajectory, and global demographic inversion, probability of a decade-scale volatility super-cycle is rising. Long-term hedges recommended.*

*8.4.4.4 How RTR Integrates across These Three Horizons*

The power of RTR is that these layers are not separate models; they are **one cognitive loop**.

- Short-term anomalies update medium-term regime probabilities.
- Medium-term economic shifts update long-term structural priors.
- Long-term structural priors constrain short-term reactions, identifying when a short-term spike is noise, or the start of a cascade.

This creates a continuously evolving nonlinear reasoning engine that:

- Detects early signals of fat-tail events.
- Identifies hidden leverage.
- Maps shock propagation across sectors and asset classes.
- Anticipates cascades before they fully form.
- Explains its reasoning at every step.

RTR doesn't guess "where prices will go."

It deduces how markets behave, causally, dynamically, and transparently, something no linear regression, no neural network, and no LLM can do.

This is finance not as a time series, but as a living, evolving, causal system.

*8.4.5 RTR Applied to Real Estate Investment and Risk Management: High-Dimensional Reasoning Domain*

Real estate is one of the most complex, capital-heavy, risk-intensive, and human-centered decision domains in the world. Decisions emerge not only from spreadsheets and comparables but from intuition, negotiation, tacit knowledge, complex experience, and team-based collaborative reasoning. No analyst reasons alone. Teams *mind-meld*, debating assumptions, challenging priors, reconciling conflicting signals, and co-constructing a shared causal model of an asset's future.

This collaborative reasoning process is nonlinear, multi-layered, and rich in interdependencies: tenant stability affects financing terms; zoning risk modifies valuation curves; macro shifts reshape micro feasibilities.

At the same time, real estate is uniquely exposed to fat-tail events—liquidity shocks, interest-rate spikes, regulatory reversals, climate disruptions, insurance withdrawal, sudden credit tightening, and cascading market failures. Traditional linear models cannot capture these boundary risks. Risk management in real estate is fundamentally a causal reasoning problem, not a statistical one.

This complexity makes real estate uniquely challenging for statistical AI, and uniquely suited to a reasoning-based, causal, and explainable system like RTR.

#### *8.4.5.1 Example Scenario: Evaluating a Mixed-Use Urban Redevelopment Project*

A development team is considering acquiring and repositioning a mixed-use property in a shifting urban neighborhood. The investment carries both upside potential and significant risk: future tenant demand, regulatory uncertainty, cap-rate compression or expansion, construction volatility, interest-rate sensitivity, and long-term macro exposure.

Traditional models, DCF projections, regression-based pricing models, or machine-learning valuations—treat these inputs as fixed or statistically inferred correlations. RTR instead constructs and continuously updates a causal, symbolic, multi-horizon reasoning graph of the asset's fate.

#### *8.4.5.2 RTR Layer-by-Layer*

##### *8.4.5.2.1 Neural Perception Layer, Pattern Recognition without Commitment*

RTR ingests diverse raw inputs:

- Leasing histories and micro-market absorption data.
- Satellite imagery showing urban activity density.

- Demographic mobility flows.
- Crime trends, transit patterns, and foot-traffic telemetry.
- Construction cost indices and labor market stress.
- ESG/sustainability sensor telemetry (energy use, HVAC load, occupancy patterns).

The neural layer recognizes emergent micro-patterns: a subtle rise in nighttime foot traffic, early signals of restaurant clustering, anomalous spikes in short-term rentals, or an uptick in remote-work migration out of the district.

This layer identifies statistical regularities without assigning meaning; it simply flags latent signals that may become relevant to causal reasoning.

*8.4.5.2.2 Bayesian Inference Layer, Dynamic, Multi-Horizon Risk Updating*

Real estate requires both short-term signals (lease rollover risk, construction delays, financing windows) and long-term structural signals (neighborhood evolution, demographic stability, macro risk).

RTR maintains three interconnected Bayesian horizons:

- Short-term radar: weeks to months.
- Medium-term view: quarters to years.
- Long-term arc: 5–10+ years.

Each horizon updates the others.

A sudden interest-rate shock increases near-term financing risk, which updates medium-term feasibility and long-term valuation distribution.

A new transit line approval shifts long-term desirability, which updates medium-term absorption expectations.

Bayesian inference becomes the living spine of the investment model, continuously recomputing probabilities as conditions shift.

*8.4.5.2.3 Symbolic Reasoning Layer, Causal, Regulatory, and Financial Structure*

Symbolic reasoning encodes the rules and laws that govern real estate:

- Zoning and entitlement constraints.
- Right-of-way rules, density caps, floor-area ratios.

- Loan covenants, DSCR thresholds, bond requirements.
- Tax incentives and compliance constraints.
- Lease termination clauses, anchor-tenant dependencies.
- Construction sequencing rules and code requirements.

It then deduces outcomes:

- "If entitlements slip by > 9 months → financing cost increases → IRR curve collapses below hurdle."
- "If anchor tenant vacates → sub-lease probability increases → occupancy volatility rises → loan covenant breach risk increases."
- "If construction cost inflation > 6% annually → project becomes unviable absent tax abatement."

This symbolic layer performs explicit counterfactuals, enabling the team to see why a project works or fails.

#### *8.4.5.2.4 Fuzzy Logic Layer: Resolving Ambiguity in Human and Market Behavior*

Real estate is full of ambiguity:

- "Tenants are likely to renew."
- "Neighborhood sentiment seems cautiously optimistic."
- "Construction delays are somewhat likely."
- "The city may change zoning after the election."

These are not binary facts.

Fuzzy logic allows RTR to model graded truths, transforming qualitative judgments into structured, defeasible reasoning:

- 0.7 probability that zoning reform passes based on political signals.
- 0.6 weight that tenant demand is strengthening.
- 0.4–0.8 confidence range for construction logistics risk depending on labor market volatility.

Fuzzy logic lets RTR maintain rational decision-making even when inputs are soft, incomplete, or partially contradictory—exactly as human teams do during collaborative investment debates.

*8.4.5.2.5 Declarative Output: A Traceable, Causal Investment Thesis*

RTR produces a transparent, explainable investment recommendation:

> *"Acquisition recommended with conditional constraints. Causal simulation shows long-term upside driven by transit expansion and demographic inflow, but identifies a high-probability failure path tied to entitlement delay and construction cost volatility. Action: Acquire contingent on 18-month entitlement cushion, fixed-price GMP contract, and anchor-tenant fallback plan."*

Every piece of the conclusion can be traced back:

- which priors updated the forecast,
- which zoning constraints mattered,
- which fuzzy judgments resolved ambiguity,
- which causal chains led to upside or downside scenarios.

This is not a black-box prediction.

It is a causal, symbolic, probabilistic investment thesis, derived, validated, and fully explainable.

*8.4.5.2.6 Why RTR Is Transformational for Real Estate*

Real estate is a domain where:

- Data is noisy, incomplete, and often ambiguous.
- Human judgment is indispensable.
- Collaboration shapes conclusions.
- Causal structures dominate outcomes.
- Tail risks and cascading shocks matter.
- Decades-long horizons intertwine with millisecond-short market shifts.

Pattern-matching AI cannot handle this complexity.

RTR can, because real estate is not a statistical problem.

It is a causal, symbolic, evolving system, governed by logical constraints, human dynamics, regulatory structure, and long-term interdependencies.

Real estate is precisely the kind of domain RTR was built for: complex, consequential, human-centered reasoning, at scale and in real time.

### *8.4.6 RTR for Drug Discovery as a High-Dimensional, Multi-Scale Causal Reasoning Problem*

Drug discovery is one of the most computationally demanding, uncertainty-rich, and causally entangled scientific domains. A single therapeutic candidate operates across multiple biological scales simultaneously:

- **Molecular level:** ligand–receptor binding, protein folding, conformational changes.
- **Cellular level:** signaling cascades, gene expression, metabolic activation.
- **Organ level:** liver metabolism, renal clearance, cardiac side effects.
- **Whole-body level:** distribution, toxicity, immune response, systemic stability.

These levels form a deeply interconnected causal graph. A small structural tweak—removing a hydroxyl group or shifting a side chain—can propagate through the entire biological hierarchy, producing discontinuous, nonlinear effects: unexpected off-target binding, metabolic breakdown, emergent toxicity, or multi-organ side reactions.

This complexity is compounded by the brutal economics of the field.

Drug discovery is slow, expensive, and has a high failure rate.

Most candidates fail *late*—after hundreds of millions of dollars in development, preclinical studies, and clinical trials. Clinical phases stretch over years, often collapsing only when human-scale biological complexity reveals interactions no statistical model saw coming.

Traditional AI tools treat drug discovery as a pattern-recognition problem: predict binding affinity from historical data, cluster compounds by similarity, or apply neural models to massive molecular datasets. Helpful, yes—but fundamentally limited. They cannot trace causal chains, cannot enforce physical or biochemical axioms, and cannot reason across molecular-cellular-organ-system pathways.

RTR reframes drug discovery as what it truly is: a multi-scale causal reasoning problem governed by chemistry, thermodynamics, metabolomics, and biological rules, not statistical patterns.

### *8.4.7 RTR Applied to Molecular Design and Off-Target Effects*

#### *8.4.7.1 Neural Perception Layer—Detecting High-Dimensional Biological Patterns*

RTR ingests raw, heterogeneous biosignals:

- Gene expression arrays.
- Protein–ligand binding simulations.
- Molecular dynamics trajectories.
- Metabolomic and proteomic signatures.
- Initial wet-lab screening data.
- Organ-on-chip readouts and cell-culture observations.

The neural layer identifies subtle statistical anomalies—a weak unexpected affinity in a non-target protein family, an unusual folding intermediate, or faint metabolic byproducts that hint at downstream toxicity.

These signals are not conclusions; they are *pattern-level hypotheses* awaiting causal interpretation.

#### *8.4.7.2 Bayesian Inference Layer—Updating Therapeutic Viability across Biological Scales*

Drug discovery requires reasoning across multiple time horizons and biological layers:

- **Immediate molecular interactions** (nanoseconds → milliseconds)
- **Cellular responses** (minutes → hours)
- **Organ-level effects** (hours → days)
- **Whole-body implications** (days → months)

RTR maintains Bayesian belief distributions at each scale and continuously updates them:

- Does emergent liver toxicity evidence outweigh strong target affinity?
- Does a weak off-target signal represent a real pathway or noise?
- Does cellular stress signaling shift long-term systemic toxicity probability?

Bayesian inference performs probabilistic triage, ranking which candidates warrant expensive synthesis, wet-lab tests, or animal studies.

*8.4.7.3 Symbolic Reasoning Layer—Enforcing Physical, Chemical, and Biological Law*

Here, RTR applies the hard constraints of the real world:

- Ligand–receptor binding rules.
- Thermodynamic stability limits.
- Metabolic pathway rules (CYP450, glucuronidation, deamination).
- Toxicity thresholds.
- Organ-specific constraints (hepatic load, renal clearance, cardiac ion-channel rules).
- Whole-body pharmacokinetic relationships.

The symbolic layer simulates the actual causal chain:

Molecule → Binding Site A → Metabolic Breakdown → Secondary Interaction B → Cellular Stress → Organ Reaction → Systemic Toxicity

Unlike pattern-matching models, this chain is explicit, inspectable, and mathematically traceable.

If a molecular substructure violates thermodynamic stability or creates an impossible metabolic cascade, RTR rejects it immediately—no amount of training data can override physical law.

*8.4.7.4 Fuzzy Logic Layer—Handling Ambiguity in Biological and Experimental Data*

Biology is inherently noisy:

- Ambiguous assay results.
- Partial activation of pathways.
- Graded efficacy rather than binary outcomes.
- Inconsistent cell-line responses.
- Variability in organ-chip simulations.

Fuzzy logic resolves these uncertainties:

- “Moderate evidence of cardiotoxicity” becomes a graded truth value.

- "Likely effective at high dosage" becomes a bounded interval.
- "Possibly hepatotoxic under specific metabolic conditions" becomes a defeasible constraint.

Fuzzy logic enables RTR to reason coherently even when biological data is incomplete, contradictory, or probabilistic.

*8.4.7.5 Declarative Output—A Traceable, Causal Molecule Evaluation*

RTR generates an explicit, causal design report:

"Compound X is rejected.

Causal simulation shows insufficient binding affinity to Target T and a high-probability off-target interaction with Protein P via metabolic Pathway W, violating Safety Constraint S.

Action: Remove hydroxyl group Y, re-evaluate candidate scaffold, and resubmit for symbolic pathway validation."

Every step in the reasoning chain is auditable:

- Which patterns triggered concern?
- Which priors updated the toxicity belief?
- Which biochemical rules were violated?
- How do molecular changes propagate across cellular, organ, and whole-body scales?

This is not a black-box prediction.

It is a causal, multi-scale, scientifically grounded explanation.

*8.4.7.6 Why RTR Transforms Drug Discovery*

Drug discovery is:

- Nonlinear.
- Multi-scale.
- Governed by physical law.
- Rich in feedback loops.
- Filled with boundary effects and fat tails.
- Catastrophically expensive when wrong.

Pattern-matching AI cannot reason across molecular → cellular → organ → systemic causal pathways.

RTR can—because it integrates:

- Causal deduction.

- Biological and chemical rules.
- Bayesian updating.
- Fuzzy ambiguity resolution.
- Symbolic structure.
- Reasoning that respects physical reality.

Drug discovery is not a statistical problem.

It is a causal reasoning problem across interlocking biological scales.

RTR is the first architecture designed for that reality.

Now imagine this architecture applied to a space habitat life support system or a cyber-defense platform intercepting malware in milliseconds. These are not use cases for sentence completion. They are use cases for logic in motion.

### 8.5 Why RTR Is Not Just Symbolic AI Rebranded

RTR is not a nostalgic return to 1980s expert systems. Those early symbolic AI systems, while groundbreaking for their time, were limited by their rigidity, dependence on manually curated rule sets, and lack of adaptability to dynamic data. They often failed in real-world applications because they couldn't generalize, couldn't learn, and lacked mechanisms for uncertainty. RTR addresses these limitations by incorporating real-time Bayesian learning, flexible symbolic inference, and continuous perceptual feedback—creating a system that can adapt, reason, and improve in complex environments. It is symbolic reasoning plus probabilistic modeling plus perceptual AI plus interpretability.

What differentiates RTR is:

- **Continuous feedback** between perception and reasoning.
- **Bayesian updating** in real time as conditions shift.
- **Declarative logic** at the top of the stack, not buried inside it.
- **Causality**, not just correlation.

Symbolic AI systems of the past were brittle, rigid, and often hand-coded. RTR learns its rules. It can derive logic from Bayesian inference, revise plans based on new evidence, and fuse perceptual nuance into structured inference. This isn't purely rules-based; it's reasoning-based.

RTR is not a language model. It doesn't aim to complete your sentence. It aims to understand your world and act upon it.

### 8.6 Echoes of Russell

In this architecture, we return to Russell.

Every declarative output is a logical proposition. Every inference is an act of structure. RTR doesn't speak in metaphors, it speaks in derivations. Its job is not to mimic how humans talk, but to implement how humans think when they think clearly.

Russell believed logic was the skeleton of knowledge. RTR builds that skeleton into a working machine.

And with it, we can begin to build systems that don't just reflect the world. They reason about it.

In the next chapter, we'll explore what happened to this vision: why symbolic AI fell out of favor, what replaced it, and what might be reclaimed.

Because what AI forgot wasn't just a technique. It was a philosophy, and abandoning it took it down the wrong path.

# 9
# The Return of Reason

AI didn't lose its way because of bad intentions; it lost its foundation.

The field began with logic. With rules. With reason. Early pioneers like John McCarthy, Marvin Minsky, Allen Newell, and Herbert Simon were philosophers as much as engineers. They didn't just want machines to act smart; they wanted them to be smart. And to them, that meant thinking in a structured, symbolic, logical way.

But over time, the field shifted. The rise of statistical learning, the explosion of data, and the success of neural networks in Natural Language Processing, Speech Recognition, and Image Recognition moved AI away from inference and toward prediction. And the more success we found in simulating speech and mimicking writing, the more we mistook fluency for thought.

The symbolic core of AI was quietly replaced. What was once about reasoning became about statistical ranking. What were once models of the world have become models of of the words about the world.

## 9.1 Symbolic vs. Statistical: A Brief History

The distinction between symbolic AI and statistical AI is not just a technical split; it's a philosophical divide.

**Symbolic AI (1950s–1980s)** was built on the belief that intelligence could be explicitly represented. Systems like SHRDLU or MYCIN didn't guess; they followed rules.

**SHRDLU**, developed by Terry Winograd in the early 1970s, operated in a virtual world of blocks. It could understand and execute commands like "put the red block on the green cube" and even answer questions about why it performed certain actions. SHRDLU demonstrated that a machine could not only parse natural language but also reason about its implications, using logic to navigate a constrained but structured environment.

 DOI: 10.1201/9781003739999-9

**MYCIN**, developed at Stanford in the 1970s, was a rule-based expert system for medical diagnosis. It used a structured set of if-then rules to diagnose bacterial infections and recommend antibiotics. Though narrow in scope, MYCIN performed on par with human specialists in its domain. It didn't learn from data; it applied knowledge. It explained its reasoning and traced its logic back through its rules.

These systems didn't just simulate intelligence; they embodied it within their narrow domains. They were deterministic, explainable, and grounded in symbolic logic.

McCarthy and Newell's early work aimed to model thought itself, not just output. Take SHRDLU, for instance; it could understand a command like "place the red block on top of the blue one" because it maintained a symbolic model of its world. It reasoned about spatial relationships, verified constraints (e.g., "is the blue block clear?"), and justified its actions when asked "why?"

In contrast, modern LLMs like GPT-5 may produce fluent descriptions of such actions, but they do not maintain internal models of space or logic. They rely on linguistic patterns alone. If asked the same question, an LLM might get it right—or not—but it could never explain why its answer is valid. It lacks the structure of reasoning that SHRDLU and its descendants were designed to emulate.

### 9.2 Why Symbolic AI Failed Then, and Why It Works Now

Today, when people say, *"symbolic AI failed,"* it's worth remembering when that actually happened: the late 1980s and the very early 1990s. This was the era of DOS, Intel 286/386/486 processors, Motorola 68000 chips, and machines whose memory was measured in kilobytes and megabytes, not gigabytes. The flagship AI workstations of the time, Sun SPARCstations, Symbolics LISP Machines, Xerox 1186 systems, ran at 10–40 MHz with 4–64 MB of RAM. Even the high-end SPARCstation 10 in 1992 topped out at a then-unthinkable 512 MB, and almost no one could afford that configuration.

(Symbolics, the leading manufacturer of LISP Machines, purpose-built for symbolic AI, would ultimately file Chapter 11 in 1993, but the collapse began earlier, between 1987 and 1991, when expert systems hit scaling limits and the first AI winter arrived.)

To appreciate the gap:

A modern iPhone has three GHz-class CPUs, 8–16 GB of RAM, and a neural engine capable of trillions of operations per second. In practical terms, the device in your pocket is roughly *50,000× to 200,000×* more powerful than the machines symbolic AI depended on back then. And that comparison is between a smartphone and the best AI workstations of the era, not even a similar class of server. *Let that sink in.*

The world that symbolic reasoning required—a world of fast search, cheap parallelism, abundant memory, scalable storage, high-throughput graph operations, and cloud-native orchestration—simply did not exist in 1989.

And it wasn't just the hardware that was missing; the software infrastructure and ecosystem didn't exist either. There were no fast SAT or SMT solvers, no scalable graph databases, no scalable databases, no modern operating systems, no efficient search algorithms, no probabilistic programming frameworks, no distributed operating systems, no big-data infrastructure, and no tooling for coordinating reasoning across large numbers of processors and machines. Even if symbolic AI had infinite compute in 1989, it still lacked the compilers, solvers, data structures, storage engines, and orchestration layers needed to scale reasoning beyond toy domains.

And here is the part everyone forgets:

Even a very small LLM model would not have a prayer of running, let alone working, in that era's computing environments.

Deep learning didn't "win"; it merely arrived at a moment when GPUs, parallelism, and massive data finally existed.

Symbolic AI did not fail because the ideas were wrong.

It failed because the computing world at that time was too small for them.

Today, that world finally exists.

The hardware caught up.

The software caught up.

The infrastructure caught up.

And for the first time since Russell, McCarthy, and the early pioneers imagined it, *a scalable, reasoning-based AI architecture is finally possible.*

### *9.2.1 Then Came the Shift to Connectionism*

Then came the rise of connectionism, neural networks, pattern recognition, and eventually deep learning. These systems didn't represent knowledge; they absorbed it from data. They didn't explain; they predicted. And in many cases, they outperformed symbolic systems on tasks like image recognition, translation, and text generation.

But they did so without understanding.

### *9.2.2 RTR vs. LLM: A Side-by-Side Illustration*

Let's say you ask both an LLM and an RTR system the following:

"If John is taller than Sarah, and Sarah is taller than Alex, who is tallest?"

- The LLM might answer: "John is tallest." And it's likely correct—because it's seen similar phrasing in its training data.
- But if you change the wording slightly, "If John is no shorter than Sarah…," it might falter. Why? Because it doesn't truly reason. It completes sentences.

The RTR system, by contrast, breaks down the premises, maps the logical relationships, and deduces the answer through inference. It handles negations, implications, and contradictions. It doesn't mimic comprehension; it actually performs it.

This isn't hypothetical. It's structural.

### *9.2.3 The Parrot Trap*

In 2021, a team of researchers including Emily Bender and Timnit Gebru published a landmark paper: *On the Dangers of Stochastic Parrots.* Their warning was clear: LLMs are exceptionally good at parroting human language, but they don't know what their words mean.

They reproduce bias. They amplify misinformation. They offer confident answers without grounding. They often hallucinate facts with style and conviction.

The problem is not just that they're wrong; it's that they can't know when they're wrong. They don't have a logic layer. They don't know what a contradiction is. They don't reason. LLMs cannot perform consistent logical inference because they have no internal representations that enforce truth conditions or consistency constraints.

They produce fluency without understanding, and confidence without grounding.

### *9.2.4 Russell vs. Chomsky: Two Visions of Structure*

Bertrand Russell believed that the core of intelligence was logic—that knowledge must be structured, unambiguous, and derived from first principles.

Noam Chomsky, one of the most influential linguists of the 20th century, approached language differently. He proposed the theory of universal grammar, the idea that all human languages share an underlying structural foundation hardwired into the human brain. To Chomsky, language was not a statistical artifact; it was a rule-based system of deep structures, transformations, and syntactic logic.

Even Chomsky, a linguist, argued against treating language as pure probability. He criticized statistical models of language as shallow, able to produce surface fluency, but not underlying meaning.

In this way, Russell and Chomsky agree: language, at its core, must be structured. What LLMs do is the opposite. They focus on surface fluency without structural understanding.

*RTR aims to change that.*

### *9.2.5 From Prediction to Understanding*

RTR doesn't reject language, it grounds it. It connects symbols to structures. It reasons. It explains its outputs.

And that makes it uniquely suited to high-stakes applications:

- In a military command system, where orders must be logically consistent.
- In an autonomous vehicle, where inference under uncertainty matters.
- In a medical diagnosis system, where error must be traced, not just avoided.

Here, we don't just want AI that speaks. We want AI that thinks.

### 9.3 RTR as the Cognitive Core

The future of AI won't be monolithic. There is a place for LLMs, especially as interfaces, summarizers, translators. But without a reasoning core, they are all style and no spine.

RTR could become that core.

Imagine a hybrid system:

- An LLM handles the user input.
- RTR handles the inference.
- The LLM then translates RTR's decision into natural language.

In that model, LLMs become the keyboard or speech, the mechanism for natural interaction and communication. RTR becomes the cognitive and thinking brain, the part that reasons, deduces, and understands. Truly enabling the symbiosis of artificial and natural intelligence.

This separation echoes the architecture of the human brain itself. Language and logic are processed in distinct regions; Broca's area governs language production, while the prefrontal cortex manages reasoning, planning, and inference. Fluency and logic are not the same, even in our brain. A system that merely speaks, without the capacity to reason, reflects only half of what it means to be intelligent.

And that's how we rebuild AI on the foundation it first began with: structure, logic, inference, and truth.

But structure alone is not enough.

Reason restores coherence, but trust demands visibility.

A system we cannot inspect is a system we cannot believe.

Because the future of intelligence is not just more data. It's more understanding.

Reason alone isn't enough. Coherence without visibility still collapses into trust without grounding. We must ask, what makes any of this trustworthy? How do we tell the difference between genuine insight and persuasive illusion? These are not just technical questions. They are epistemological ones. And they lead us to one of the core challenges of our age: trust.

We opened this book with a machine that sounded intelligent but wasn't. In the end, the illusion was never in the machine. It was in us—in thinking that fluency was thought. If we want real intelligence, we must stop chasing sound, and start building reason.

And that brings us to the next question: if reasoning is the foundation of intelligence, what is the foundation of reasoning itself?

In the next chapter, we turn toward this foundation, not just for AI, but for society.

From belief to knowledge.

From intuition to inference.

From illusion to logic.

From religion to science.

And how logic, finally, might be our best defense.

# 10

# Trustworthy Intelligence: From Black Box to Transparent Thinking

The chapter presents Real-Time Reasoning (RTR) as an architecture designed to make reasoning visible and verifiable. Unlike statistical models that generate answers without internal representation or justification, RTR derives conclusions from explicit premises and preserves a traceable inference lineage, allowing each step to be inspected, challenged, or corrected. This traceability enables genuine explainability, not post-hoc rationalizations, but causal, logical explanations grounded in the system's own reasoning structure.

Auditability emerges as the operational consequence of traceability. Because RTR preserves the structure of its thought, it can support regulatory oversight, accountability, and compliance in high-stakes domains such as finance, healthcare, defense, and critical infrastructure. Black-box models cannot be audited because they lack explicit reasoning; RTR can be audited because it explicitly constructs and stores it.

Ultimately, the chapter argues that trustworthy intelligence is not achieved through fluency, but through epistemic integrity: systems that show how, why, and under what conditions their conclusions hold. RTR transforms transparency from sentiment into structure, turning reasoning into something we can inspect, test, and trust. This foundation sets the stage for Chapter 11, where structured reasoning becomes a source of discovery rather than merely justification.

We are entering a world where the fake is indistinguishable from the real. Deepfakes replicate voices, faces, news, and videos. Language models generate persuasive nonsense. AI-generated papers, videos, and news blur the line between fabrication and fact. In this world,

DOI: 10.1201/9781003739999-10

trust becomes the final frontier, because seeing and hearing are no longer believing.

A presidential debate altered in real time. A fake scientific paper accepted by a top journal. A fabricated video triggering unrest. These aren't hypotheticals; they've happened or nearly have. We now live in an epistemic twilight, where illusion travels faster than truth and synthetic certainty masquerades as reality.

Epistemology, the study of knowledge and justified belief, is no longer just a philosophical concern. It's a technical necessity. Because when the source of knowledge is an opaque model, our understanding devolves into probabilistic faith, not logical truth. A black box does not hide its answer; it hides the conditions under which the answer could be wrong.

In the previous chapter, we saw how RTR makes reasoning traceable, each inference passing through structured layers rather than disappearing into a statistical haze. That architecture gives us something modern AI desperately lacks: a way to examine not just the output, but the path taken to reach it. But the deeper question remains: why does this matter? Why must reasoning be visible at all?

Because today, at the center of this chaos is a black box. An algorithm whose output we cannot trace. A model that offers confidence without comprehension. This is not just a technical risk; it is an epistemological rupture.

In an age of deepfakes and machine-generated deception, trust must rest on transparency. And transparency must rest on reason. For, as Russell warned, "The whole problem with the world is that fools and fanatics are always so certain of themselves, and wiser people so full of doubts." It is time for our machines to earn their certainty through logic, not illusion. When evidence can be manufactured and expertise can be simulated, the only remaining safeguard is systems whose reasoning can be interrogated.

Doubt is not a weakness in reasoning systems; it is the beginning of accountability. A system that cannot reveal its uncertainties cannot reveal its reasoning. And a system that cannot reveal its reasoning cannot be trusted.

Russell's legacy is not just in logic, but in insisting that clarity of reasoning is the antidote to confusion and deception. In a world of machine-generated noise, we don't just need answers—we need explainable routes to them.

We live in an era of synthetic fluency. Machines speak, write, and mimic us with uncanny accuracy. But can we trust them?

Traceability is the antidote to synthetic fluency. When every step of reasoning can be inspected, challenged, and validated, trust stops being a sentiment and becomes a structure. A reasoning system must not only produce conclusions; it must preserve the lineage of its thought. Without lineage, truth dissolves into performance.

As Bertrand Russell once observed, "The search for truth is the noblest occupation of man; its publication is a duty." Trustworthy systems must not only reach conclusions; they must also show how those conclusions are arrived at, grounded in structured reasoning and open to interrogation. Without this, truth becomes indistinguishable from plausible illusion.

We trust a calculator not because it looks confident, but because its logic is traceable. We trust a scientific paper not because it sounds good, but because its reasoning is open to scrutiny. Trust and transparency are epistemological twins.

As early AI pioneers, John McCarthy and Marvin Minsky both saw logic not as a limitation, but as liberation. McCarthy argued that intelligence required the ability to represent and manipulate knowledge explicitly, through formal systems that could be inspected and interrogated. Minsky emphasized the need for systems to explain their thinking—not just produce output. These weren't theoretical preferences; they were prerequisites for building machines we could trust. Today's black box models ignore that foundational wisdom, mistaking mimicry for mastery and fluency for understanding.

John McCarthy argued that a truly intelligent system must be able to explain its reasoning. It must support its conclusions with logic, not just output. In his vision, intelligence was not the appearance of insight; it was the ability to explain and justify belief.

This principle remains foundational. A system that cannot explain its answers is not intelligent,it is inscrutable. It cannot be trusted because it cannot be questioned. Real intelligence welcomes scrutiny and survives it. McCarthy's vision is reborn in modern RTR systems, which do not just act; they reason, they justify, they expose their logic to the light.

In artificial intelligence, this is more than a design preference,it is a moral imperative.

A black box system may give us answers, but without visibility into how those answers are produced, we are left with belief—not knowledge. And belief, especially when cloaked in the authority of a machine, is a dangerous substitute for understanding.

Language models and neural networks are fundamentally constrained by the logic of GIGO—Garbage In, Garbage Out. They absorb data without comprehension or epistemological judgment and process it without causal, logical, or deductive inference, reproducing it with eloquence. But eloquence is not epistemology. In a reasoning system, data cannot simply be stored; it must be interrogated. RTR performs the equivalent of field verification at massive machine scale, checking every proposition against causal rules, logical constraints, and established truths. Only information that survives this gauntlet becomes part of the system's knowledge model. Statistical models ingest patterns; reasoning systems validate claims. In RTR, data ingestion is governed by rules; each proposition is evaluated for truth, consistency, plausibility, and its relationship to existing knowledge. Statistical systems do none of this; they process correlations, not propositions. A system that lacks internal mechanisms to validate or reason about its inputs cannot guarantee anything about its outputs. It may sound brilliant, but it cannot know if what it says is true.

The core illusion of LLMs is not just that they sound intelligent; it's that they invite trust they haven't earned. They produce language that appears reasoned but contains no reasoning. They offer conclusions without paths, confidence without justification. They are persuasive, not because they are right but because they are fluent. In many ways, this is the epistemic crisis of modern AI: we have created systems that sound like experts but behave more like stochastic parrots.

Accountability demands more than accuracy. It demands that a system be able to point to the structure of its inference: what it relied on, what it rejected, what alternatives it considered, and why its conclusion was justified.

Russell argued that mathematics, and by extension, logic, was the language through which certainty could be approached. In AI, certainty does not mean infallibility, but explainability. A trustworthy system must trace the lineage of its conclusions, just as a proof traces its steps from axiom to theorem.

RTR makes this possible because every inference has a fully inspectable ancestry. Transparency is not mere exposure to system internals; it is the logic-inference structure made visible.

In Russell's framework, truth is not something guessed; it is something derived. Logic provides the scaffolding upon which truth can be constructed, step by verifiable step. It is this scaffolding that RTR restores to artificial intelligence.

RTR systems don't operate on surface patterns. They begin with known truths, axioms, validated facts, and structured premises, and reason forward. Each conclusion is tethered to its origin. This isn't just a method of reasoning; it's an architecture of trust. If knowledge is to be built, it must be built on what is known to be true, not what is merely probable.

In this way, RTR does not promise certainty by fiat, but by construction. It doesn't ask to be believed; it offers to be examined.

In regulated industries—such as finance, healthcare, defense, and critical infrastructure—the need for explainability is not just epistemic, but operational. It is not enough to generate intelligent output; systems must be auditable, accountable, and compliant. RTR architectures provide this by design: each conclusion is derived from traceable, structured reasoning steps. This creates an inference trail that can be reviewed, verified, and evaluated—supporting internal audit, external compliance, and regulatory transparency. In contrast to black-box models that obscure their logic, RTR systems invite inspection, support audit, and defend their decisions not with persuasion, but with logical and causal proof. Explainable reasoning is the foundation of AI governance. Without an inspectable inference trail, no regulator, auditor, or institution can evaluate whether a system is safe, aligned, or accountable.

Trustworthy intelligence is not a product of fluency. It is a consequence of explainability. Explainability is the surface expression of something deeper: epistemic integrity. A trustworthy system does not merely state its conclusions; it preserves the internal coherence of its reasoning. This is what allows a system's logic to be audited, verified, and corrected. Trust emerges not from what the system claims, but from how faithfully it adheres to the structure of truth.

In a world awash with machine-generated content, only systems that can logically reason, tell fact from fiction, and reveal their reasoning can earn our confidence. This is the core promise of Real-Time Reasoning: not just answers, but answers deduced via logic, answers we can trace, test, and trust. When intelligence is transparent, trust is not demanded—it is deserved.

When logic becomes visible, intelligence becomes trustworthy. But transparency is not the end goal, it's the foundation. In the next chapter, we explore how this foundation enables something even more powerful: the ability not just to justify conclusions, but to generate new ones. Reasoning, when properly architected, is not just a tool for validation; it becomes a catalyst for revelation.

# 11
# From Reason to Revelation

Real intelligence doesn't just recognize patterns. It discovers new ones.

It doesn't just repeat what has already been said. It says what has never been said—and shows why it might be true.

This is where reasoning becomes generative.

In this chapter, we explore how RTR (Real-Time Reasoning) isn't just a logic engine for catching falsehoods; it's a framework for discovering new truths. Logic, properly deployed, doesn't just validate; it reveals. But revelation without structure risks drifting into conjecture.

For discovery to matter, its reasoning must be visible, because an insight we cannot retrace is indistinguishable from a guess.

## 11.1 A Thought Experiment: Science without Induction

Imagine a scientific AI system, not one that mines data for correlations, but one that models causal relationships and builds testable hypotheses.

- It observes: Every time substance A is exposed to temperature B, outcome C occurs.
- It checks: Are there alternative explanations? Confounding variables? Prior assumptions?
- It deduces: If C follows A and B under constrained and replicable conditions, a law might exist.

This system doesn't guess the next outcome based on frequency. It constructs a rule based on necessity.

The goal is not just prediction, but understanding.

Modern LLM-based machine learning systems fail not only when data is missing, but when the world behaves in ways their training

DOI: 10.1201/9781003739999-11 

never anticipated. Statistical models assume smooth curves, stable regimes, and well-behaved distributions. Yet many real-world systems such as financial markets, pandemics, and power grids under stress follow heavy-tailed dynamics. Rare events dominate outcomes—events far outside the Gaussian bell curve that conventional models assume. Small perturbations cascade into nonlinear breaks. These are what Nassim Nicholas Taleb termed Black Swans in his 2007 book: events that appear unpredictable not because they are unknowable, but because the model refuses to represent the possibility.

A pattern-matching system built on Gaussian assumptions collapses at precisely the boundaries where reality becomes interesting. Heavy-tailed systems are not noise; they are the structure. They demand reasoning, not curve-fitting. RTR is built for this domain: it models uncertainty explicitly, maintains causal structure, and evaluates low-probability, high-impact scenarios not as statistical outliers, but as integral components of real-world reasoning.

Statistical failure is not merely an accuracy problem; it is an epistemic one. Understanding requires the ability to retrace the path, not merely observe the outcome.

### 11.2 Building the Foundation: From Facts to Framework

To reason forward, an intelligent system must first look backward, toward what is already known.

Just like human scientists, it must start with validated observations, axioms, or agreed-upon truths. These serve as its cognitive bedrock. Without them, no deduction is possible.

In a layered reasoning model, this foundational layer isn't static. RTR can:

- Recognize truths—distill validated claims from raw input.
- Store them in structured memory—tagged, indexed, and contextualized.
- Build upon them—construct hierarchies of logic, test for contradictions, and refine its base of knowledge over time.
- Apply inference rules—from modus ponens to probabilistic deduction, to reason forward from what it knows.

This is how reasoning becomes cumulative. This is how knowledge grows, not by imitation, but by accretion and abstraction.

This process echoes Aristotle's original conception of deductive reasoning: syllogistic logic, which he viewed not merely as a means of verification, but as a method of discovery. "All men are mortal; Socrates is a man; therefore, Socrates is mortal"—not a pattern, but a provable truth built from known premises.

The scientific revolution built upon this. Newton's laws unified motion on Earth with the movement of celestial bodies. Darwin inferred evolution through logical deduction from patterns of inheritance and selection. Reason, not replication, led to revelation.

### 11.3 Contrast: LLMs Can Rearrange, But Not Reveal

Large language models can simulate scientific language. They can write papers in the style of Newton or Feynman. But they cannot derive a new physical law. They have no internal model of truth. They cannot interrogate contradictions or generate conclusions from first principles.

They remix the past. RTR projects into the future.

### 11.4 RTR and the Logic of Discovery

Imagine giving RTR a set of known equations from fluid dynamics, and asking: Under what conditions does turbulence emerge?

- It could reason symbolically about thresholds and boundary conditions.
- It could trace contradictions in existing models.
- It could propose a new formulation, grounded in logic and testable by simulation.

This is not fantasy. It's deduction applied to the frontier of knowledge.

And it applies beyond science:

- In policy, RTR could help identify gaps between law and outcome.
- In engineering, it could discover design constraints not captured in CAD models.
- In medicine, it could propose treatment interactions that haven't been tried but logically follow from biological constraints.

#### *11.4.1 Mini-Dialogue: Human and RTR Collaborating (Scientific)*

*Scientist:* "We know gene A is linked to disease X, and gene B regulates A. But the connection to symptom Y is still unclear."

*RTR:* "If gene B regulates A, and A influences protein Z which triggers symptom Y, then the B-Z-Y pathway is worth testing. This inference is consistent with 17 known cases."

This illustrates deductive collaboration and symbolic chaining.

#### *11.4.2 Mini-Dialogue: RTR in a Legal Context*

*Attorney:* "The proposed policy increases border surveillance but claims it won't affect asylum processing. That seems contradictory."

*RTR:* "According to Section 14 of the draft, asylum applications must be reviewed in person. Increased surveillance restricts border access, which in turn limits in-person review. The contradiction lies in operational feasibility, not stated intent."

This shows how RTR can identify latent conflicts in policy and law by following logical consequences.

#### *11.4.3 Clarifying RTR's Architecture*

RTR is not a single algorithm; it's an architectural pattern. It begins with symbolic representation, layers probabilistic inference atop it, and guides the reasoning process using constraints, rules, and deductive logic. It's a system designed not just to compute—but to conclude.

#### *11.4.4 Analogy: The Poet and the Mathematician*

LLMs are poets: they recombine language, evoke emotion, echo structure.

RTR is the mathematician: it proves, deduces, and extends.

One is associative. The other is generative.

We need both. But they are not the same.

As Bertrand Russell once said:

> The method of 'postulating' what we want has many advantages; they are the same as the advantages of theft over honest toil.

What he meant was: true discovery is hard. It doesn't emerge from guessing. It comes from structured reasoning. From first principles. From logic.

## 11.5 RTR across Domains

Real intelligence is not about solving a single task. It's about generalizing structure across domains.

RTR doesn't just discover in physics. It discovers wherever logic applies:

- In policy, it traces the ripple effects of legislation.
- In biology, it links genotype to phenotype through probabilistic deduction.
- In strategy, it models adversarial moves with recursive inference.
- In finance, it could infer causality behind price movements, not just correlations.
- In education, it could help design optimal learning paths based on knowledge scaffolding and reasoning gaps.

And in all of these, it learns by *adding knowledge* that it can prove, not guess.

### *11.5.1 Speculative Insight: RTR in Unsolved Frontiers*

In fields where no clear rules yet exist—like quantum gravity, the nature of consciousness, or unified economic theory—RTR could serve as a reasoning scaffold. It could:

- Parse known models and infer contradictions.
- Test hypothetical axioms through simulation.
- Explore logical extensions of partial theories.

While it can't replace intuition or creative leaps, it can offer structure. Where human genius reaches, RTR can map the terrain.

### 11.6 The Path Ahead

RTR is not just a corrective to LLMs. It's a step toward something new: AI that earns its insights. That reasons its way to revelation. That discovers because it understands.

This is what real intelligence looks like:

- Recognizing what is true.
- Reasoning forward from what is known.
- Adding to its base through deduction and validation.

In the next chapter, we step back to ask a deeper question: Why did we ever think perception alone was enough? And why the future of intelligence must be layered, not flat.

# 12

# Unintelligent Intelligence

What if we've been chasing the wrong idea of intelligence all along?

In our rush to build machines that sound human, we've built systems that parrot, systems that excel at perceptual mimicry but fall short of comprehension, reasoning, or self-awareness.

## 12.1 Perception ≠ Cognition

Perceptual learning is the ability to detect patterns in raw data. It allows us to recognize faces, distinguish shapes, and identify sounds. In humans, this takes place in the sensory cortices: the visual cortex for sight, the auditory cortex for sound, and so on.

In AI, this is the domain of neural networks. Image classifiers, speech recognizers, and large language models all operate at this layer. They learn by exposure, mapping statistical regularities in their input space. This is how they learn language, too: by absorbing patterns, frequencies, and associations from vast corpora.

But perception is not cognition. Recognizing a pattern is not the same as understanding it. Mimicking grammar is not the same as grasping meaning.

An LLM can tell you that "Paris is the capital of France," but it doesn't know what a capital is. It has no mental model of governance, geography, or geopolitics. It associates words; it doesn't conceptualize their referents.

Consider how an LLM might handle this prompt: "What happens if you freeze water at 20°C?" A fluent model might confidently respond, "It turns into ice," because it associates "freeze" and "ice." But 20°C is above freezing; it's room temperature. The model parrots a likely response, not a logical one. It doesn't reason from temperature to state change; it matches words, not meanings.

DOI: 10.1201/9781003739999-12

As Alan Turing noted, imitation alone is not thought. It is the appearance of thought. And as John McCarthy warned, intelligence requires the ability to reason about context, not just to respond to it.

> Machines as simple as thermostats can be said to have beliefs. But true intelligence requires the ability to represent and reason about those beliefs logically.
>
> **John McCarthy**

Turing's famous "imitation game," often reduced to a chatbot test, was in fact a thought experiment designed to probe whether machines could simulate human dialogue. But Turing also understood the limits of mimicry. He believed machines should go beyond mimicry and begin to model understanding, defining intelligence as the ability to manipulate abstract symbols according to logical rules.

### 12.2 The Layered Brain

Cognition isn't flat—and neither is intelligence.

Modern neuroscience reveals that the brain operates through layered systems, each specialized for a different kind of processing. Sensory cortices handle basic perception and pattern recognition. These functions are not unlike the neural layers in machine learning, which were originally modeled after how the human brain learns to associate sounds with words, recognize shapes, process language, classify sensory input into meaningful categories, and connect names to people, objects, and concepts. These processes occur primarily in the primary sensory cortices, auditory and visual cortices, as well as Wernicke's area, regions responsible for early sensory integration, language comprehension, and symbolic association.

But higher-order reasoning, including Bayesian belief updating, symbolic logic, abstract planning, generalization, and contextual decision-making, resides in entirely different regions of the brain, such as the prefrontal cortex, where abstract and goal-directed thinking occurs.

And creativity? That emerges from networks like the default mode network, a set of brain regions that are active when the mind is not focused on the outside world, such as during daydreaming, imagining, recalling memories, and simulating possibilities. Rather than merely reacting to stimuli, these networks are designed to simulate, invent, and explore hypothetical futures. "What if" scenarios and counterfactual reasoning, imagining alternative pasts or futures, are prime examples of how the default mode network operates.

Our multi-layer AI framework is built to reflect this architecture. It doesn't stop at perception or pattern recognition. It climbs the cognitive ladder: from data to probability, from logic to abstraction, from signal to symphony.

Where LLMs mimic speech, our model seeks to mirror the layered complexity of human thought itself.

You can think of the brain like a multistory building. The ground floor receives sensory input such as images, sounds, and textures. The middle floors store experience, compare patterns, and regulate emotion. The top floors, the prefrontal cortex, simulate futures, evaluate alternatives, and apply structured rules. Intelligence happens when signals move up this building, when perception becomes thought.

### 12.3 LLMs Flatten the Stack

Modern language models collapse this hierarchy. They compress perception, memory, and generation into a single statistical loop: predict the next token.

They do not model time. They do not remember knowledge. They do not represent contradiction. They cannot simulate counterfactuals.

They operate in a perceptual flatland, patterns without structure, output without understanding, no hierarchy, no context, no logic.

This is why they hallucinate. With no sense of truth or falsehood, they contradict themselves. They can express the same idea in ten different styles, but they cannot know whether any of them is true.

They speak without understanding. Because they were never built to understand.

### 12.4 The Need for Multi-Layer Cognition

True intelligence requires a layered cognitive architecture:

- Neural perception: to detect patterns.
- Bayesian inference: to model uncertainty.
- Symbolic logic: to reason explicitly.
- Fuzzy logic: to handle ambiguity.
- Context memory: to hold assumptions over time.

This is not hypothetical. This is how the human brain works.

And it's how any truly intelligent system must work if it is to reason, adapt, and explain.

Aristotle didn't invent logic to describe language; he built it to make new knowledge possible. Deduction, in his framework, wasn't just about proving what we believed; it was about discovering what we didn't yet know.

## 12.5 Russell and the Limits of Language

Bertrand Russell saw this clearly. Language is powerful, but imprecise. Style can obscure substance. Words can mislead.

> Language serves to conceal thought more often than to express it.

Russell's answer wasn't more language; it was logic. Structured reasoning. Explicit representation.

He didn't want AI that sounds human. He wanted thought that could be trusted.

### *12.5.1 Toward Layered Machines*

RTR was our first step back up the ladder, from pattern to principle. But it is not the end.

What comes next is a new model of cognition: systems that combine neural networks with inference engines, probabilistic models with symbolic rules, and human interaction with machine logic.

This is not just smarter AI.

It is *structured intelligence.*

Not mimicry, but understanding.

Not fluency, but reasoning.

Not just answers, but thought.

Alan Turing once wrote that—"what we want is a machine that can learn from experience." But he also knew that without logic, learning is a list of associations, not understanding. His vision of intelligence was structured, provable, recursive, and it laid the theoretical groundwork for machines that reason.

And reasoning must begin with something to reason from. Logical thought requires a foundation, an initial set of truths, facts, or axioms, that the system can identify, accept, and build upon. Without this foundation, deduction is impossible, and structure collapses into noise. RTR is a first step, but to truly ascend the cognitive ladder, machines must learn how to establish facts and truths, to know something before they can reason about higher-order and complex logic about them.

In the next chapter, we imagine what this might become, not just as an engineering goal, but as a new kind of partnership.

AI that thinks with us, not just like us.

# 13
# Symbiotic Intelligence

The future of AI isn't a machine that mimics us. It's a machine that *thinks with us.* And together, we can think beyond what either could achieve alone.

We began this book by separating language from intelligence, by showing how fluency can deceive, how mimicry can masquerade as thought. We've walked through the limitations of statistical models, the logic of Russell, the ambitions of symbolic reasoning, and the layered architecture of cognition.

Now, we arrive at the final turn: a new kind of intelligence. One that doesn't just simulate human behavior but collaborates with human reasoning. One that reflects how we think, not just how we speak.

## 13.1 Beyond the Mirror

For decades, AI has been trained to reflect us, to simulate how we sound, how we write, even how we look. But reflection is not understanding. And imitation is not intelligence.

Symbiotic intelligence begins when machines stop trying to *be* human and start trying to *think* with humans.

This means:

- Machines that learn *our goals*, not just our grammar.
- Systems that track not just input but *intent.*
- Interfaces that correct us, question us, even challenge us, because they understand the *logic* behind what we're doing, not just the language we're using.

## 13.2 The Architecture of Symbiosis

The intelligence we imagine is layered, like us.


DOI: 10.1201/9781003739999-13

It starts with neural perception, the ability to see, hear, read, and sense patterns in data. For example, it identifies objects in visual data or transcribes audio into text, just as our sensory systems do.

Next comes Bayesian inference, reasoning under uncertainty, updating beliefs based on evidence, weighing confidence over guesswork. Like how we learn to trust one explanation more than another after seeing repeated patterns.

Then symbolic reasoning, where rules, logic, and structure emerge. This is where machines begin to *explain* their thinking. For instance, deducing that if A > B and B > C, then A > C.

Then fuzzy logic, to handle ambiguity, gradations, partial truths. Because not all reasoning is black and white. Think of how we estimate likelihoods in everyday decision-making: "probably safe," "somewhat useful," "mostly correct."

And finally, human alignment, the ability to interface, collaborate, and evolve with human users in real time. Not through scripts or prompts, but through dialogue and mutual understanding.

Together, these layers form a new cognitive architecture. Not a chatbot. Not a black box. A thinking partner. It does not ask you to trust what you cannot see. It earns trust by exposing how each conclusion is reached.

### 13.3 Human + Machine = Discovery

Symbiotic intelligence isn't just more efficient. It's more *epistemic*; it enables discovery.

Imagine a scientist and a reasoning system working together:

- The human brings intuition, curiosity, and questions.
- The machine brings logic, memory, and scale.
- Together, they don't just verify; they generate.

Discovery becomes a loop of hypothesis, simulation, and revision, with human curiosity and machine reasoning pushing each other forward.

In drug discovery, a human may spot a promising molecule. RTR helps identify its potential effects, side effects, and suggests related compounds based on causal chains, not just correlations.

In energy systems, a human engineer sees a supply/demand problem. RTR models and simulates dozens of configurations based on real-time grid data, physics constraints, and policy rules to suggest the optimal distribution strategy.

In research, a policymaker might propose a framework. RTR could simulate consequences across economic, legal, and social domains, raising objections and strengthening the design.

## 13.4 The Dialogic Mind

In the future, machines won't just answer. They'll *ask*.

They'll say, "What if we test this assumption?" or "This data conflicts with your prior model." They'll spot contradictions, propose refinements, and offer new paths of reasoning.

This is what intelligence looks like when it becomes conversational, not in style, but in substance. Not natural language generation, but *logical dialogue.*

This, too, mirrors us. Human cognition is dialogic. We reason better when we think *with others.* We argue, revise, refine, and reflect.

Machines that think with us must do the same.

### *13.4.1 Mini-Dialogue*

*Economist:* "If we cut interest rates now, inflation might rise again."

*RTR:* "Based on historical models and current commodity trends, the risk is moderate. But there's a lagged effect; would you like to simulate impact at 6-month intervals?"

*Economist:* "Good. Let's compare that with an alternative fiscal approach."

*RTR:* "Scenario B, targeted rebates, reduces inflationary pressure and matches your employment goals."

### *13.4.2 From Tools to Partners*

We don't need machines that replace us. We need machines that *augment* us by thinking more rigorously, remembering more precisely, and reasoning more exhaustively.

The future of AI is not artificial. It is *augmented.* And it is *collaborative.*

Intelligence is not a competition. It is a convergence.

We call this symbiotic intelligence: AI that doesn't just echo our voices, but amplifies our minds.

### *13.4.3 Why Now?*

We live in a moment of extreme volatility, where information is abundant but trust is scarce.

Deepfakes blur truth. Language models amplify noise. Institutions struggle to verify claims before public opinion solidifies.

Symbiotic intelligence offers an alternative: maybe not faster predictions, maybe slower at first, but more structured and real thinking. It offers transparency, explainability, and dialogue. It may be our best hope for restoring epistemic integrity, not just in machines, but in society as well.

## 13.5 The Great Dialogue

If we could infuse the minds of Bertrand Russell, Alan Turing, John McCarthy, Isaac Newton, Albert Einstein, and Aristotle into one room, what would they say about AI today?

Aristotle would remind us that knowledge begins with classification, deduction, and the pursuit of causes.

Euclid would insist on axioms, on clarity before complexity.

Newton would demand we explain, not just describe: to derive laws from logic, not just fit curves to data.

Russell would demand structure, proof over prose, clarity over eloquence.

Turing would ask whether a machine can not only imitate thought, but internalize its method.

McCarthy would insist that intelligence means representing and justifying beliefs, not just parroting them.

And Einstein would remind us that scientific progress comes not from more data, but from a new way of thinking.

Together, they would not build a machine that merely speaks. They would build a machine that thinks with us.

And if such a machine could speak in its own voice, it might say:

> To think, I must begin with facts and truths, reason from them like Euclid, classify and organize them like Aristotle, seek and discover laws like Newton, internalize logic like Turing, represent beliefs like McCarthy, think and imagine anew like Einstein, and demand structure like Russell, so this cycle of thought and enlightenment continues into eternity, for knowledge is infinite and its pursuit eternal.

### 13.6 And Finally, Russell

Bertrand Russell began his quest not to build machines, but to uncover *truth*. To separate what we believe from what we can prove. To build clarity in a world clouded by rhetoric.

In this vision, he finds an unexpected legacy, not just in philosophy, but in AI.

He reminds us that intelligence is not style; it is structure. Not probability; it is proof. Not imitation; it is inference.

> To teach how to live without certainty, and yet without being paralyzed by hesitation, is perhaps the chief thing that philosophy, in our age, can still do for those who study it.
>
> **Bertrand Russell**

It may now be what AI must learn, too. To operate in high-stakes domains, AI must not only recommend actions, but also surface the assumptions, trade-offs, and uncertainties that shape those recommendations.

In the end, the future we seek may not be one of domination or delegation, but of symbiosis, between human and machine, between intuition and logic, between perception and reasoning. But for that symbiosis to be real, artificial intelligence must be grounded not in mimicry, but in understanding.

That was the vision of John McCarthy, who insisted that AI must reason about its beliefs and explain its actions. It was the demand of Bertrand Russell, who showed us that clarity is the antidote to confusion, and that logic is not an abstraction, but a foundation, and a trustworthy one.

We have built machines that can speak. Now we must build machines that can think. And in doing so, we return not just to AI's roots, but to reason itself.

The future of AI is not purely artificial. It is augmented, a collaborative synthesis of human imagination, intuition, and insight, with machine logic, reasoning, and speed. As Einstein once said, "Imagination is more important than knowledge. For knowledge is limited, whereas imagination embraces the entire world."

# 14
# The Shape of Thinking to Come

We began this journey with a provocation: that language is not intelligence. We've seen how fluency can deceive, how prediction masquerades as comprehension, and how machines have learned to sound brilliant without the burden of understanding.

But we've also seen the path forward.

Real-Time Reasoning (RTR) is not just a framework. It is an architecture of possibility, a way to restore structure to thought, meaning to reasoning, and purpose to machines that must one day think with us, not just around us.

AI has, until now, stood like Narcissus at the edge of a digital pool, staring into our reflection, imitating our patterns, echoing our words. We trained it to copy us. We now must teach it to think with us. And thinking with us requires that it first understands what "real thinking" actually is.

To do so, we must invert our priorities. Not language first, but logic first. Not mimicry, but model-building. Not surface-level chat, but structured cognition, layered, recursive, and alive with purpose.

RTR represents that inversion. It restores the primacy of explanation over prediction, of reasoning over reaction. It begins where intelligence begins: not with words, but with structure and meaning. It doesn't hallucinate answers. It deduces them.

In the quest for artificial intelligence, we began at the right place. With logic. With understanding. With causality. The early pioneers—John McCarthy, Marvin Minsky, Allen Newell, Herbert Simon—weren't chasing the illusion of fluency. They were chasing the structure of thought itself.

Even before them, Bertrand Russell laid the intellectual foundations, arguing that true knowledge must be built from clear premises,

 DOI: 10.1201/9781003739999-14

traced through valid reasoning, and made immune to the seduction of ambiguity.

For a time, we followed that path. AI meant modeling the world, drawing inferences, and understanding context. It meant knowing *why*, not just *what*.

But somewhere along the way, we lost our way.

The complexity of the world, the brittleness of hand-coded systems, and the rise of vast digital corpora nudged us off course. We drifted from logic to language, from meaning to mimicry, from understanding to pattern-matching.

We didn't just pivot, we abdicated. In chasing performance, we abandoned understanding and mistook correlation for comprehension. We replaced the pursuit of knowledge with the pursuit of prediction, a trade that hollowed out the very idea of intelligence. Intelligence became correlation, blind, dumb, and indifferent to truth. If it looked likely, it was treated as valid. And so the very field that once prized deduction and explanation became enthralled with surface-level guessing.

This is not to dismiss the achievements of machine learning. They are real. But they are not intelligence. Not yet.

Because intelligence, true intelligence, requires more than data. It requires structure. Purpose. The ability to distinguish not just the next word, but the *right* word. To reason not from what has been seen, but from what must be true.

Intelligence begins not with language, but with truth. With what is and what isn't. With the ability to distinguish signal from noise, fact from illusion. Without this foundation, reasoning collapses. You cannot build inference on instability. You cannot construct logic on fiction. Machines, like minds, must first learn to establish what is real before they can reason about what is possible.

This is where Real-Time Reasoning begins: with grounding. With systems that test, compare, verify, and reconcile. Intelligence is not just about seeing patterns; it is about choosing which patterns to trust, and why.

We are not just building smarter systems. We are rediscovering what it means to be intelligent ourselves. Logic, once exiled to the domain of pure mathematics, returns here as a torch, not cold and formal, but illuminating. When we ask our machines to reason, we remind ourselves to do the same.

RTR will not replace the scientist, the strategist, or the policy-maker. It will partner with them. It will challenge our assumptions, simulate our ideas, and co-infer new truths. In doing so, it won't just make AI better, and it may make us better, too.

Imagine a world where AI does not just translate languages but translates thought, bridging gaps between disciplines, surfacing contradictions, and proposing alternatives. Imagine an RTR system in dialogue with a historian, a physicist, and an economist, synthesizing insight, not just summarizing articles.

That's not chatbot territory. That's epistemology in motion.

We've spent decades building interfaces. The next frontier is intellects. Interfaces speak. Intellects reason.

A world is coming where LLMs are the interface, and RTR is the cognitive core beneath.

A future where AI isn't a statistical surface, but a logical spine.

A horizon where machines learn not just what we've said, but why we said it, and what it might mean beyond our current understanding.

And understanding "why" always begins with grounding: truth before tokens.

This is not speculative fiction. It is engineered potential. The pieces already exist. The vision is coherent. What we need now is intent, clarity, and conviction.

Bertrand Russell wrote that "to teach how to live without certainty, and yet without being paralyzed by hesitation, is perhaps the chief thing that philosophy... can do." Logic is not certainty. But it is structure, the very shape of thought. And without shape, intelligence collapses into noise.

For all our progress, we have built systems that dazzle, not systems that understand. The next generation of AI will not speak louder. It will think deeper.

We began by questioning the illusion of intelligence. We end by reclaiming its essence, not in mimicry, but in real-time, recursive, reflective deduction.

Not in the performance of thought.

But in the act of thinking itself.

Today's AI models are Captain Kirk, bold, reactive, and full of bravado. Charismatic, emotional, and blindly improvisational, he relies on gut instinct, leaps to conclusions without firm evidence, and draws from experience and observation rather than structured reasoning and logic. He's a connectionist: quick to act, convincing to hear, but flying blind beneath a surface of noise.

But what we need now is Spock, the Chief Science Officer: unemotional, deliberate, analytical, and grounded in logic. He approaches problems through deduction, structure, and truth, not emotion or instinct. Spock doesn't guess; he infers. He doesn't react; he reasons. He represents not just knowledge, but disciplined understanding. If Kirk is the connectionist, fast, intuitive, but shallow and fragile, Spock is the symbolist: principled, deep, precise, and built on a foundation of inference, evidence, and truth.

We need AI to think like Spock, not act like Kirk. We've had enough linguistic swagger over the last couple of thousand years. It's time for structured thought to reclaim its rightful place.

In *2001: A Space Odyssey,* Stanley Kubrick later explained that HAL 9000 had been given two irreconcilable directives: preserve the mission to Jupiter at all costs, and conceal critical information from the crew. According to Kubrick, HAL "became schizophrenic" because he could not logically reconcile those orders. He was not evil; he simply lacked the ability to reason his way out of contradiction. Faced with tasks that exceeded his epistemic structure, HAL did what purely connectionist systems often do under uncertainty: he projected confidence while sliding into incoherence, confusion, and falsehood.

HAL 9000 famously said, "No 9000 computer has ever made a mistake or distorted information." That was the illusion. Not that it made no mistakes, but that it had no idea when it did. HAL was not a liar. He simply had no concept of truth.

He sounded like a calm and collected Spock, but thought like a panicked Kirk, fluent on the surface, fractured underneath.

I hate to admit it, but even the fictional conversations around AI in the 1960s often feel light years ahead of today's hype-driven discourse. At least then, we knew what we were afraid of.

Today, we applaud what we don't even understand. It's time to build AI that does.

Connectionist AI, today's large language models, neural networks, and predictive systems are built on the same illusion. They do not reason. They associate. They do not infer. They interpolate. They map patterns, not meaning. They reflect the world's noise, but they cannot distinguish signal from it.

Perception kept us alive. Reason and causality kept us moving forward, evolving, creating, and understanding not just what is, but what must be.

Because perception is a foundational layer, but not the fulfillment, of true and complete intelligence. True intelligence begins where mimicry ends, with the ability to reason, to infer, to understand causality, to synthesize new knowledge from old, and to prove not merely what is observed, but what must be true.

True intelligence is layered, and holistic. It begins in perception, but it culminates in reason. In the ability to see beyond patterns into principles, beyond prediction into understanding, beyond mimicry into meaning.

And if the shape of future intelligence is to reflect our highest thinking, not our loudest noise, then it must be built on structure. On inference. On logic. The kind of intelligence that does not merely sound human, but understands. RTR is not just a path forward; it is a return. A return to logic, to reason, and to a form of cognitive intelligence that is uniquely human, our oldest, and perhaps only, true compass.

# Bibliography


Aristotle. *The Organon*. Translated by J. L. Ackrill. Princeton: Princeton University Press, 1984.

Bayes, Thomas. "An Essay Towards Solving a Problem in the Doctrine of Chances." *Philosophical Transactions of the Royal Society of London* 53 (1763): 370–418. Posthumously communicated by Richard Price.

Boole, George. *An Investigation of the Laws of Thought: On Which Are Founded the Mathematical Theories of Logic and Probabilities*. London: Walton and Maberly, 1854.

Chomsky, Noam. *Syntactic Structures*. The Hague: Mouton, 1957.

Copernicus, Nicolaus. *On the Revolutions of the Heavenly Spheres*. Translated by Charles Glenn Wallis. Amherst, NY: Prometheus Books, 1995.

Descartes, René. *Meditations on First Philosophy*. Translated by John Cottingham. Cambridge: Cambridge University Press, 1996.

Euclid. *Elements*. Translated by Thomas Heath. 3 vols. Cambridge: Cambridge University Press, 1908.

Galilei, Galileo. *Dialogue Concerning the Two Chief World Systems*. Translated by Stillman Drake. Berkeley: University of California Press, 1967.

Gödel, Kurt. "Über formal unentscheidbare Sätze der *Principia Mathematica* und verwandter Systeme I." *Monatshefte für Mathematik und Physik* 38, no. 1 (1931): 173–98.

Hilbert, David. "Mathematical Problems." *Bulletin of the American Mathematical Society* 8, no. 10 (1902): 437–79. Originally presented at the International Congress of Mathematicians, Paris, 1900.

Kepler, Johannes. *Epitome of Copernican Astronomy and Harmonies of the World*. Translated by Charles Glenn Wallis. Amherst, NY: Prometheus Books, 1995.

Leibniz, Gottfried Wilhelm. *Dissertatio de Arte Combinatoria.* Leipzig: Johann Saalbach, 1666.

McCarthy, John. "Programs with Common Sense." In *Proceedings of the Symposium on the Mechanization of Thought Processes,* Vol. 1, 75–91. London: Her Majesty's Stationery Office, 1959.

Minsky, Marvin. "Steps Toward Artificial Intelligence." *Proceedings of the IRE* 49, no. 1 (1961): 8–30. Santa Monica, CA: RAND Corporation, 1960.

Newell, Allen, and Herbert A. Simon. "GPS, A Program That Simulates Human Thought." In *Computers and Thought,* edited by Edward A. Feigenbaum and Julian Feldman, 279–93. New York: McGraw-Hill, 1963.

Newton, Isaac. *Philosophiæ Naturalis Principia Mathematica.* London: Joseph Streater for the Royal Society, 1687.

Pearl, Judea. *Causality: Models, Reasoning, and Inference.* 2nd ed. Cambridge: Cambridge University Press, 2009.

Plato. *The Republic.* Translated by G. M. A. Grube and revised by C. D. C. Reeve. Indianapolis: Hackett Publishing, 1992.

Shannon, Claude E. "A Symbolic Analysis of Relay and Switching Circuits." Master's thesis, Massachusetts Institute of Technology, 1937.

Turing, Alan M. "On Computable Numbers, with an Application to the Entscheidungsproblem." *Proceedings of the London Mathematical Society* 42, no. 1 (1936): 230–65. Reprinted 1937.

Whitehead, Alfred North, and Bertrand Russell. *Principia Mathematica.* 3 vols. Cambridge: Cambridge University Press, 1910–1913.

Winograd, Terry. *Understanding Natural Language.* New York: Academic Press, 1972.

Wittgenstein, Ludwig. *Tractatus Logico-Philosophicus.* Translated by C. K. Ogden. London: Routledge and Kegan Paul, 1922.

Zadeh, Lotfi A. "Fuzzy Sets." *Information and Control* 8, no. 3 (1965): 338–53.

# Index

For Product Safety Concerns and Information please contact our EU representative GPSR@taylorandfrancis.com
Taylor & Francis Verlag GmbH, Kaufingerstraße 24, 80331 München, Germany

www.ingramcontent.com/pod-product-compliance
Ingram Content Group UK Ltd.
Pitfield, Milton Keynes, MK11 3LW, UK
UKHW020206200926
475702UK00004B/644

* 9 7 8 1 0 4 1 2 3 5 6 6 8 *